GROUP CONSCIOUSNESS

Group Consciousness

Realizing Brotherhood on Earth

White Eagle

White Eagle Publishing Trust

NEW LANDS · LISS · HAMPSHIRE

www.whiteaglepublishing.org

First published 2016

© Copyright, the White Eagle Publishing Trust, 2016

British Library Cataloguing-in-Publication Data
A catalogue record for this book is available
from the British Library

ISBN 978-0-85487-241-1

Set in 13 on 14.5 pt Perpetua at the Publishers
and printed in Great Britain by
the Halstan Printing Group, Amersham

Contents

About this Book

'GROUP CONSCIOUSNESS' is the point in human evolution when souls allow their own needs to be absorbed into the needs of the group. In short, a feeling arrives that other humans genuinely are our brothers and sisters, and all life seems part of that same continuum. Thus, in describing the foundation of brotherhood on earth, White Eagle directs us to look towards an eventual state of oneness with all life. He uses the word 'brotherhood' not as in a this-world phrase such as 'the brotherhood of man', but as something that involves a shift of consciousness, so that in embracing the quality of brotherhood, the seeker is also raising his or her consciousness into an awareness of every dimension of life – across every universe and from the beginning to the end of time – as one whole.

It's hard, for this reason, to limit the term with a formula that reflects duality, such as 'brother–sisterhood', however much we might like to hear that in preference to the seemingly gender-specific word. We ask every reader to extend their imagination to allow this. There is no gender at all in the way White Eagle refers to 'brotherhood', and it includes things that have no gender in English: rocks, stars, angels and plants, for instance. Sometimes, of course, White Eagle does use 'brother–sisterhood', but in the very gentle editing of White Eagle's live talks that is involved in the compiling of this book, we have permitted ourselves to regard the terms 'brotherhood' and 'brethren' as non-gender-specific, while making sure that the simple word 'brothers' (which might seem particularly specific) is accompanied by 'and sisters' every time it appears. Never, in any circumstances, does White Eagle speak of one sex as having precedence over the other. Moreover, his frequently poetic words always carry more meaning than their literal sense.

This book thus offers us a conscious opportunity to develop group awareness at a soul level and so enable greater service to all humanity and to the divine principle. 'Brotherhood' therefore means something else still, beyond what was implied at the start of this introduction. From the start of his work, White Eagle guided his medium, Grace Cooke, into forming an actual, physical, group of committed pupils whom he called his 'Brotherhood'. That group first met in February 1934 and still meets today; it seeks, through its coming together, to imitate the model of an enlightened brotherhood in spirit, sometimes referred to as 'the Brotherhood of the Light', or 'of the Star', or 'the White Brotherhood'.

In the text, words like 'brotherhood' are capitalized when they refer specifically to this Brotherhood at either level, and uncapitalized when they are used generally. The word 'master' is another example, where the specific generally refers to the Master Jesus. White Eagle is frequently at pains to remind us that there are female 'masters' as well as male: the word 'mistress' is not available to describe them.

In the text, the brotherhood on earth that White Eagle began is generally the audience to whom the teaching in this book was given. Sometimes White Eagle speaks very generally, and truly everything in this book is selected to apply to groups of committed light workers right across the globe. Every now and again, though, the intimacy of the speaker within his circle of listeners, which by design has never been allowed to grow large, comes across clearly. If ever the reader feels this little circle or 'lodge' is being highlighted above others, he or she should hear our editorial assurance that White Eagle would always prefer inclusion to exclusion, and would invite every reader to feel truly welcome within the group, in spirit at least. The whole book is really an attempt to share the experience of brotherhood as actually lived by the White Eagle Brotherhood.

It is hoped that something else comes across. People qualify themselves for the joy of service in brotherhood by understanding and commitment; we have already used the word 'initiation' to describe the process (not at the earthly level so much as at the spiritual one) by which a soul is led into service to humankind in stages. Once dedication is given in brotherhood or in service to the light, it is not broken without sadness. Thus the individual needs to be very sure of the path to which he or she commits. Every reader of this book, however, is entrusted with the information and teaching that it contains. As you read it, we invite you to go imaginatively into the circumstances in which the teaching was given, and recognize the dedication the then hearers had already given in order to be present in the circle. The book will mean more to you if you take it slowly, a little at a time, as a pupil of the teacher – just as the original hearers were trained, week by week.

The name of Grace Cooke was mentioned as White Eagle's medium, and all the teaching in the book came 'through' her, in trance, at Brotherhood meetings (there are a very few exceptions, when the teaching was given to a wider audience). The name by which many people knew Grace Cooke was 'Minesta', and the co-founder of the White Eagle Brotherhood at the earthly level was her husband and partner, Ivan, generally known by the name White Eagle used to address him, 'Brother Faithful'. He is mentioned on p. 180.

Lest it might seem that brotherhood can be achieved overnight, let it be said that the formative years of the White Eagle Brotherhood, the 1930s, were fraught with all sorts of difficulty; this Brotherhood was certainly not formed without birth pangs and growing pains. Next the world plunged into war, and from this period quite a number of the passages in this book have been selected. Perhaps only because of those difficulties in infancy, though, has it been strong enough to survive through to to-day, steadily growing. Its ambitions are only those of service, and are exactly as set out here.

Mentioning actual brethren is intended to help the reader appreciate the commitment others have shown and to remember that all that this book offers is about the voluntary service of actual individuals. The seed for it was a collection of White Eagle 'brotherhood teachings' specifically on this subject, which was begun by Minesta's daughter Ylana Hayward. She was one of the very first brothers (yes, she would have endorsed that term warmly!) initiated in 1934 – not actually by White Eagle, but by the messengers of the Polaire Brotherhood in Paris, from whom our brotherhood mission derives, though the connection was deliberately broken before the Second World War. We know that those referred to would all describe their dedication to the brotherhood above as something that brought infinite joy as well as hard work.

It also is a reminder that the raising of one being through aspiration and service is a raising of all other beings, too. One of White Eagle's favourite sayings is from chapter 12 of St John's Gospel, *I, if I be lifted up from the earth, will raise all men unto me*. He refers to this saying more than once. There is a long tradition, going back to early times, which relates this not to the crucifixion but to an elevation of an individual's consciousness that opens his or her vision to all levels of life, and that is how White Eagle interprets it. The power the one has (or the few have) to lift the many is the rationale behind commencing brotherhood within a small group. As the consciousness of the few grows, so does the brotherhood of all things become awakened.

A final word may serve as further reassurance to all that White Eagle's words are addressed here to all servers of the light, and not just his pupils at the time. In a teaching not reproduced in this book, he speaks of work with the light as being like a wheel, upon which we all make up the rim, but every one of us is equally attached to the hub. But the crucial words from that teaching to share are these:

'God be with you. God bless you on your journeyings. God be with you, and love, for when you love there is no separation. Spirit comes together as one whole as soon as each human being loves.'

CHAPTER 1

What All the World's Awaiting

TO HEAR the heartbeat of the universe, each being must be still. The world breathes in the breath of life from the heart of God. You may all learn the secrets of life, and the changes in form of life, if you will learn to draw aside the veil between the material and the spiritual worlds. No teacher can teach you the way, except the teacher within yourself, the teacher who stands at the altar in the centre of the temple, the teacher which is God. You, beloved, are that One. . . .

The heart of the universe beats in rhythmic song in all creation – in the song of the birds, in the perfume and colour of the flowers, in the wind in the trees, in the sky and the running water, in the sunshine and in the rain, in life and in death.

And humanity, your brothers and your sisters, are suffering in the darkness, where life is chaotic through lack of at-one-ment and harmony with the cosmic life. . . . Yet you may reach the heart of humanity so easily, and so simply. Let love take the place of fear – fear of the injury your brethren may inflict upon you, fear of the consequences of events.

Become the instrument of the divine love which was expressed in Jesus the Christ.

White Eagle's teaching comes from a higher level of life than our own, and from that perspective limitations that stand in the way of our earthly vision are removed. In the passages that follow, he is talking very simply to a small group of his devoted followers. It is noteworthy how he re-gards spirituality as learnt lessons, rather than what we might today call 'a lifestyle choice'.

You know, if you could look, without your physical vision but with your pure spiritual vision, you would see into the hearts of all men and women – and you would find, beneath all the rubble and the rubbish, a great sweetness. If you will cultivate the true vision, you will see sweetness everywhere, sweetness in all peoples. At the present time it is only God or one of the Wise Ones who can fully touch that sweetness in a human heart, but you are all being trained to do just this: to look into the darkness and see the shining light.

We have told you that the foundation of all life must be spiritual. When the foundation is rotten, the structure crumbles and falls away, or rather is carried away by a grand cosmic process. All that you have been going through in your individual lifetimes will be recognized as a spiritual foundation for the new age – laid, not by those in earthly power, but by

the ordinary people of the countries whose governments are so often in conflict. Beneath the surface,
the ordinary peoples of the world are at work. We
use this phrase to describe all those who have one
aim, one ideal, one aspiration – the simple-hearted,
pure-hearted, kindly peoples who desire peace and
brotherhood – the people with hearts of goodwill
who desire simplicity but who are ready to recognize true greatness and true leadership.

True greatness lies only *within* the man or woman
of God. No one can live in real truth while denying
the power of the one spirit of all life. You will therefore understand that what is happening at the present time is a shaking up of humanity, so that eyes
will be opened to the true harmony and wisdom of
the spiritual law. The cause of chaos is separateness.
There can be no such thing as splendid isolation, for
all are interdependent; it is a grave as well as a joyous thought that no one of you can live just unto
him- or herself.

The further the mind probes into the depths
within the soul, the more conscious the mind becomes of its kinship with other men and women.
Development of group consciousness is of the utmost importance, because this group consciousness eventually brings about God-consciousness,
or consciousness of the universal, of a wide brotherhood and an eternal life. The trouble with the

world today is lack of this group consciousness, or too much individualism; and individualism means separation, isolation. But as the soul becomes more conscious of its brothers and sisters throughout the universe, so it becomes more God-conscious, more Christ-conscious. When this ideal state of life has come into being on the earth, there will be no more material conflict. Instead of conflict there will be unity, a working together to produce and to create a more and more beautiful state of living.

The goal to which we are all working is universal brotherhood, though with earth consciousness you can catch only a faint gleam of the true state of brotherhood. You all strive to be loyal to those with whom you are joined in brotherhood, and to each other; and some of you often feel discouraged, disappointed with their efforts. This must ever be so. It is impossible for you to tread the path without enduring the disappointment of failure. We understand, beloved brethren, so well; but do not be discouraged, any one of you. In the secret chamber of your heart you know the truth.

Before you is a magnificent opportunity to help humankind. This is the way in which you can accept and make use of that opportunity. Look out into the world upon your brothers and sisters, and look for the God in them. Look for the good in all things and in all presentations of spiritual truth.

Having presented an ideal to which each of us, already but often unconsciously, may be aspiring, White Eagle begins to talk about the ways in which we might achieve the goals we have set ourselves.

How best may we help our brothers and sisters when they are in trouble, and do not understand the secret of life? Only by giving forth from the centre of our own being a loving understanding of their need, which can be done in quiet. It is unnecessary to speak to the sleeping soul, but instead silently we may express in love the help which will enfold him or her and permeate the aura of our friends. Eventually the light permeating the aura will awaken an answering note within. It is unwise to use arguments. The right thought has greater power than the spoken word ... for the right thought will encircle and penetrate the soul of every being.

The people of earth place so much trust in *doing* things! Wisdom, alone, teaches you how potent is thought, is love. God never fails, God will never fail his child, no matter how great the need, God will supply that need.

The Infinite, beloved, lies within, not outside, yourself.

*

We have told you many times that the positive good thought of one individual is more powerful than the nebulous negative thought of ten thousand. And so

17

we say, *cast out fear*. There is nothing for you to fear. Fear in the minds of men and women is a very bad thing, my children, because fear is a weakness and it is like a chink in the armour of God. If you fear anything you are making way for the enemies, the adversaries of God. Therefore when you find yourselves fearing, either about yourself, your health, your conditions or anything that comes into your life, you are weakening yourself.

Do not fear. Place your whole confidence in God, the Father—Mother. Follow God; take the gentle way; offer the other cheek; be guided by your intuition and love. You will have chosen the better path, the God path. Remember this.

It is a basic tenet of White Eagle's teaching that the beginning of all action lies in thought. Thus in seeking to build awareness of the beauty of every individual contribution to the whole of life, he suggests we begin by looking at our own thought-patterns. After thought, there are the values we set ourselves, ready to shine through our actions.

You are all instruments, receivers; not only are you receivers, but you can also be projectors of certain vibrations of sound and light. That which lies within the invisible, within the silence, must eventually be brought forth. That is what people are doing today, learning to bring forth the magic that lies within. Witness what you contend with: the cruelty, the suffering, the oppression on earth. Is it imaginable that these atrocities are being inflicted?

When you pause and think, all that you hold most sacred rises in revolt, in sorrow, and in shame. And yet, war and injustice and cruelty are born on earth as the result of *people's innermost thoughts*. That which you think today becomes a condition of tomorrow. The suffering of today is the result of the cruel, unbrotherly, selfish thoughts of yesterday. This must cause you to pause and think, to think about your very thoughts.

Are you contributing thought-substance to humanity which will be constructive and helpful in the years to come? Are you sending forth into the ether vibrations of light and sound which will ultimately find their mark? Will the human receivers change their ways? Can we inspire them to love their brethren – to serve, to understand them? This we who work with the light are all striving to do. And we who are discarnate are able to see the effect of your collective thought as it is sent forth across the world. That which lies in the invisible, and within the Silence of today, will be audible and visible to human beings tomorrow.

*

Humanity cries out in its anguish and rushes hither and thither, seeking for excitement, striving to satisfy the desires of the flesh and of the astral and lower mental vehicles. Men and women climb to great heights, seeking satisfaction through fame and self-glorification. But few enter through the narrow gate; there are few who can see the way to the eternal light. The narrow way which is spoken of by our more orthodox brethren has been spurned by the great intellects of all time, spurned by those who have sought to possess power – power to dominate their fellow creatures.

We would describe the narrow way as the simple way. It does not condemn human beings to material poverty, nor does it bar them from harmony and beauty, but it is the way which brings them harmony and abundance. It is the way of love....

You live in a chaotic, cruel world, and cruelty one towards another is one of the greatest known sins – whether cruelty to one another or cruelty to animals, cruelty to nature or cruelty to the angelic world. It is not always realized that unkind words and criticism rank as cruelty. To judge another is a form of cruelty. This cruelty must be replaced by brotherhood, by kindness; and every true brother or sister to humankind can encourage a dislike of cruelty in all its forms. We remind you that cruelty exists not only on the physical plane, but to a greater degree on the mental and spiritual plane.

Examine the question of cruelty and you will see how far it overrules human life. To turn a deaf ear to the needs and the suffering of another is cruel. Being yourself slack and indifferent concerning the feelings and sufferings of others is cruel. We all have obligations and responsibilities to our sister and brother. Those brought into our area of service need our wise supervision and help. If we do not give it to them, through our own slackness, then we are being cruel. We have an obligation to our fellow beings, and we must see to it that the obligation is fulfilled. We must examine our actions, our words, our thoughts, and see if they measure up to the standards of kindness and brotherhood.

There are many forms of life looking towards you, towards your life, to help them, even as you look towards the light which shines in the distance. God helps you; you help the lesser forms of life. The nature and animal kingdoms look towards the human for help along the path of evolution as you look forward to the angelic. Therefore we finish by impressing these thoughts upon you. You owe a responsibility to the lesser kingdoms; in every thought of love and wisdom that you radiate you are helping some younger, perhaps tiny little life-form, upwards towards the light.

White Eagle now returns to describing how in the silence we may rediscover ourselves. Here he begins by referring to one of the truly great beings who serve as our examples, and follows this example with another, that of the group that has become known as the Albigenses or Cathars. We shall return to the idea of the silence in chapter eight.

Beloved brethren, we bring you peace. Think of the great Lord Buddha, an emblem of stillness of spirit. It is the purpose of the Master to teach the brethren of the West to receive into their souls the contemplative peace which their eastern brethren have long since learnt to express and to be. In the civilizations of the past, the inner circle of initiates learnt through self-discipline to enter the inner sanctuary, the holy of holies of the temple, and to perceive the light of the star that guided them on life's way. Great wisdom came to these initiates; their wisdom came not from books, not from great intellectual attainment, but from the stillness and silence of the temple. They looked into the well of truth, and saw reflected in the water the wonder of creation and the great law which caused the great universe to become the outer expression of that innermost sacred secret of the Most High.

Many men and women seek to know the cause, the purpose, and the ultimate goal of life. Humanity can only find the answer to this problem within the sacred precincts of the temple of silence. And peace is from within. But you must also seek it from without. We mean by this, that in your earthly life you must endeavour at all times to preserve in your out-

22

er consciousness the stillness and calmness of peace; in the midst of the multitude there is peace ... but in the heart of the desert there may be tumult and storm raging within you. You know not the power which you generate by bringing the outer consciousness into subjection to the king – the spirit, reigning within you. In peace there is power, creative and health-giving. In noise and tumult there is chaos and no power, for in tumult there is disintegration.

Cultivate poise of spirit, peace of mind, and when you have the reins well in your hands, you have taken the first step towards the temple of God.

*

We would impress upon you that the brotherhood in your Middle Ages known later as the Albigenses was a brotherhood of sweetness and simplicity. They lived a communal life and were, very simply, brothers and sisters. They lived to serve their fellow creatures as you are trying to do. They received from the one you know as St John* the secret of developing those spiritual senses which enabled them to see clairvoyantly the spirit land and the spirit life. The Albigenses lived close to God and to nature and to all the angels. When they died, they were already in a state of ecstasy, and went forth into the world

*For an interesting vision which backs up this belief, see the introduction to White Eagle's book THE LIVING WORD OF ST JOHN (4th edition, Liss, 2010).

of spirit in full consciousness of the greater life, seeing the angels waiting there to receive them. You have no idea yet of the joy and the ecstasy of the spirit when as a brotherhood you can see the vast concourse of shining souls waiting for you all in the higher sphere of life.

This we want you to remember, and when you meet with those you are in harmony with at the spiritual level, try to enter into that heavenly ecstasy yourselves, and see in spirit those radiant brethren who are with you and helping you every step of the way. And what have you to do in order to qualify for this glorious experience? You have to live a simple, brotherly life: pure and whole and healthy; human, angelic – to be just dear, sweet brethren.

*

Life is brotherhood; none, as we have said, can live in splendid isolation. The whole of life is one vast brotherhood, and when the individual brother or sister puts himself or herself into harmony with the Great White Brotherhood, with the brotherhood of all life, then that person receives in full measure the abundance, the help and the power and the healing which he or she needs in life to restore harmony and to speed spiritual evolution.

Finally, White Eagle reminds us that the moment of commitment to the work of developing brotherhood is a kind of initiation in itself. He calls it the fire initiation, because it is an opening of the heart to the great wealth of love that lies therein. This passage directly addresses his own followers, once again.

To our brethren we speak with great love. In the silence of this little brotherhood all must be aware of the love of God, and of the love and wisdom of those Great Ones who live and work for the younger brethren. May every soul be raised above the smallness of the little self, and hold communion with the great, the Universal Spirit. Only in the little self are separation and fear known. Rise above the little self, and so become enfolded by the love of God, of spirit.

This is the first realization which comes to the one who passes through the fire initiation – the baptism by fire of the spirit. With the coming of this light into the soul of each being, all sense of separation vanishes. This means that as soon as the soul is baptized by the spirit, it identifies itself with every living creature, with sky and wind and rain; with tree and shrub and flower, with grass and corn; with all insects and winged creatures, with bird and animal.

My beloved brethren, when you have passed through the great initiation, the baptism of the fire of the spirit, you will be able to see with the vision of the spirit, and see in the hearts and souls of all humans the light, and the dearness and sweetness. Thus the spark within the heart will grow until it becomes a great fire, and by its light you will see the mystery of life. Is this not good to know?

*

The spiritual is more real than your physical life. You touch your chair, you feel with your physical body, and because you feel with the sense of touch you think that you touch reality, forgetting that in a few years all these things return to nothingness. But that which you use on the inner planes, the planes of spirit, will live when all around has passed, when the form that you know today is gone. The real things are those which come from your spirit, from your inner self, from the 'place of the knower'; from the knowing within you. The knower is the real, the true, the higher self – and the higher self knows truth, when the lower self denies it.

We pray that you may get increasing realization of this as you endeavour to be a true brother in all that you do and say. It is not easy, and we all make slips and mistakes; but be not daunted by these, only resolve to do better and better. And be true, *be true* to the spirit of brotherhood in life.

Humanity – God's children – will march forward. Send forth a ray of light and power until it reaches the darkest places on earth and into the spheres surrounding the earth. It will go forth, even as the Master himself still walks among the people, touching eyes sealed by blindness, making the blind see; touching hearts cold and chill like stone, and awakening them to life and beauty and love; touching misshapen bodies, causing them to be whole; touching angry hearts and causing them to turn to love; causing the nations to beat the swords and guns into ploughshares....

By this power alone, the power of the light, will humanity go forward progressively, constructively, happily....

A Meditation on the Love of God for All Life

Let us raise our consciousness above the earth, and see the radiance and glory of the heavenly spheres. We are caught up in the power, the beauty and the love. The earth life, the material life, is beneath our feet.

Feet on the earth, we know that there is only one reality, the God life. We know that God loves every part, every atom of life. We know that all life moves slowly but surely forward and upward. We know that only love is real.

We know that we are in the care of our beloved elder brethren, that we are in the heart of God. We know that as we learn the necessary lessons of life, we shall find both freedom and unity. Life is perfect law.

So may we dwell in peace: true peace of the spirit within.

LKM

CHAPTER 2

Brotherhood Comes to the Earth

In the first chapter, White Eagle presented an innate sense of their brotherhood one with another as a natural urge bringing all people closer. Generally, when speaking thus, he does not imply any degree of separation between activity at his own level of life and that which we perform on earth in imitation of the spirit life. We are all, he would say, engaged in the same principle of service to life — and service is service, wherever it takes place.

He has also identified himself as the spokesman for a specific brotherhood on a plane even higher than his own, and for the whole system he uses the term 'the White Brotherhood' — meaning, of course, nothing about the colour of their appearance except in so much as they shine with the light they embody. In what follows, 'the White Brotherhood' will sometimes imply something infinitely beyond everyday experience, and sometimes a brotherhood in which we can actually participate on earth. The level at which we participate will depend on our gradually unfolding consciousness.

MY BRETHREN, does there not sometimes come to you a sense of vast companionship? Does there not come to your heart a realization that you are not alone, that you are one of a vast company? What a comfort, what inspiration, what joy – and how the heart rejoices and gives thanks to God for sharing in this privilege of service!

Brotherhood means a sending forth of goodwill into life, *good will*. If you persistently and consistently send forth goodwill, you are acting as brethren. Our desire is to help our brothers and sisters on earth to reach their goal – not the goal of the lower self, not the realization of material ambition, but the realization of the soul's ambition, which is to become one with God, one with the will of God. We desire, then, one thing in brotherhood, and this is that through our goodwill and clear vision we may help our dear brethren on earth to reach the goal of spiritual freedom.

We know that thought is the strongest power in life, and we ally ourselves with the invisible powers, the invisible brotherhood, in streaming forth into the ether the same kind of qualities that they too continually send forth – goodwill, light, love. We know that these radiations of ours *must* reach their point, and that the accumulation of these thoughts of goodwill towards life gradually awaken, in the consciousness of our fellow men and women also, the desire to radiate goodwill. This is brotherhood: this is how we help our brethren.

There are many groups, many forms of service on earth today, political and otherwise, and, if you examine all these groups, you will find that they each have something to commend them. But apart from all these earthly groups, there is one centre of truth which all groups need to contact, and this centre is the inner group of the White Brotherhood, the group which knows one truth — goodwill towards all life. Now if these groups on the outer planes can link up with that one inner group of goodwill, then they will all be raised up into one grand brotherhood on earth.

*

My dear ones, give unto others that which you have received for yourself. There are so many who are lonely, and so little can bring the light of joy to their eyes and heart. Even the most hardened materialist is hungry — hungry and sorrowful — and the materialism is only there to cover a broken heart. Be gentle, but be persevering to get some love into the stronghold of that lonely brother or sister's life. And then, into the greater world, carry the radiation of constructive thought.

Many times White Eagle refers to 'the ancient wisdom', meaning the truth which was given to humanity at the beginning of incarnation, brought by those he elsewhere calls 'Sun Beings'. The following passage offers greater understanding of a quality which the Sun Beings by their very name manifested — the quality of light. Rather beautifully, he here links light with both silence and truth.

31

ı to the wisdom and love of the eternal light; ent wisdom is the light in humanity, but also child of the Father–Mother God. Pure truth is pure light, which is why it is not possible to clothe pure truth in words. So soon as the attempt is made, limitation comes. There are many diverse forms of teaching precisely because words and the human channel always limit the manifestation of the pure light.

In moments of silence the soul receives its own divine illumination. In the spirit world we meet in the temple of brotherhood and listen to a divine truth which enters our hearts from the eternal light. Each man and woman qualifies through service to that light to receive more and more knowledge and wisdom. This does not come through intellect only, but through growth of the light in the heart.

This is not *our* teaching, dear brethren; we are ourselves but poor instruments for that divine and glorious light. But words have to be used in an endeavour to open people's souls so that they may themselves fling wide open the door to receive the full flood of eternal truth, the divine love: the light expressed by the human heart in the form of love and service to all created things.

Always think in terms of the eternal light. When things are not easy in your lives, resign all in humility to the light. As you attune yourselves, so all good will come in you and into your lives. Thus are you freed for ever from the limitations of matter. Let us give all that lies within our hearts to further the work of the light on earth.

And so, let us give sympathy, love and friendship, brotherhood, companionship, to all creatures – human, animal, etheric. This is our work. If we allow the divine light to manifest through us into the lives of others, we are qualifying to become White Brothers in the vast temple of God's universe. Beloved brethren, when we open our hearts to this central truth we become illumined, caught up in the divine fire and freed from all the heaviness, fears and limitations of the earth. All have to rise: you who are still enslaved in the flesh, and we who are your brethren behind the veil of matter; for above and reaching down to us are beings that are infinitely lovely – they to us and we to you! Thus a vast chain is formed, and in the words of Jesus we know that if 'I' – the Christ – be raised up *in us*, all beings shall be raised. Great is our responsibility but great is the joy in this work. Let the light shine! Let us put all our efforts forth to keep the divine fires burning brightly in the four corners and in the etheric planes surrounding the earth; let our endeavours be so high that all become light incarnate!

*

There are those among you whose duty takes them among great worldliness, and they find it difficult to keep attuned with that spirit of peace and love which they know exists at all times; they are unable to realize this presence when in contact with worldly affairs. Remember, beloved brother or sister (we speak to each individual) that you may at all times keep in your heart the thought of the presence of Christ. Remember that Christ, when manifesting through the physical body of Jesus of Nazareth, would be found ever peaceful and calm amid great turmoil and worldliness.

His disciples today are seeking, and must ever seek to find, the place of quiet and sweetness in the midst of the crowd. It is easy in solitude to be close to the Christ, but the great man or woman, the tried and tested, is the one who can become aware of his or her master, despite the crowding of the multitude. This contact, which all brethren can make, is not an illusion, not merely visionary, but a scientific truth.

Remember, therefore, in the midst of turmoil that you can tune in at will to the Brotherhood and the wisdom of the ages. You can be in communion with your master, whenever you will; your master's thought will be directed to you, and if you are pure in thought, you will be able to pick up your master's ray more easily than a station on an earthly radio. Nothing, except your own thoughts, will separate you from your master, and from the centre of light which you serve.

Another concept which helps us understand how brotherhood can arise is that of the higher and lower self. These terms should not lead to a belief that one is inferior to the other – the two form a continuum – but they offer separate levels of consciousness upon which we may exist, even simultaneously. From the same principle we get the term 'the higher mind', and likewise the 'lower'.

The story of Jesus stilling the waves is from St Mark, 4:35–41.

'Seek truth!' We desire only truth; the higher mind of an individual indeed seeks truth. When we refer to the lower mind, we mean the mind usually called practical, reasonable, businesslike, worldly-wise; it all seems so very right in a practical world to follow the ordinary methods. But the lower mind is a deceiver, and leads men and women along devious paths. If the higher self is born within, and would grow and find truth and reality, a truth which will free men and women from disappointments and disillusions and sufferings, then the mind of the higher self can only attain this through humility.

It is true, as you will find when you have meditated. Your teacher within the heart centre will also tell you that only through donning the raiment of humility will you find truth. My dear ones, at times when you come up against material and human problems your natural reaction is a flaming up of the passionate emotions.

35

Such indignation sends forth into your aura the red flame of passion, and arises from the lesser, or lower, self asleep at the bottom of the craft. When the fearful disciples on the lake awoke Jesus, calling for his protection, he arose, and the storm abated.

The higher self, that which is described as the 'I am' within, may be likened to the Master sleeping in the craft; the craft being the human heart. The passions and the storms may be likened to the emotional body, to the lower self; and the soul to the disciple who would follow the directions of the Master. The disciple – the soul – calls to the Master – to the spirit, to the I AM, to the higher self – asleep in his or her heart, crying, 'Master, save us, or we are consumed by the elementals which attack us from the world of desire and passion!' And the Master within, the higher self, calls: 'Peace, be still!'

Do you not then see, beloved, that you must seek the true centre of your being through humility? For while you remain arrogant, you stand directly in the storm track. Only when you can be humble – humbled to the master, to the voice within your heart – will you find peace. Then what happens? Behold! the vision clears, the storm clouds roll away, the sky becomes blue, and the sun shines upon the everyday scene. The problems which have vexed you have all been cleared away; you realize that they have passed, having no longer power to hurt you.

Following on from this picture of the serene and humble servant of humankind is teaching in which White Eagle asserts that the clearest possible demonstration of brotherhood on earth was given in the interaction of Jesus and his disciples. The teaching of Jesus, understood with real commitment, is the foundation of almost everything that is required of us in brotherhood. In the first paragraph White Eagle is reminding his own little group of brethren how they relate to the group Jesus himself began.

All the quotations here are from St John's Gospel (chapters 11, 14 and 15), apart from one from the Psalms (Cast your burdens, Ps. 55).

We want to sow a few seeds in your heart about the ministry of the Master Jesus, the Christ. You may be conscious now of his radiance, of his glorious spirit, for he is shining upon you all. He is here with you, for together with those with whom you work you are to him a brotherhood, a young brotherhood of the Great White Light.

Jesus still lives upon earth, although not among human beings in the same way as he did when he ministered to the multitudes in his own country and taught them the age-old truth of life. As time passes it becomes ever more evident how his truth is taken by intellectual people and interpreted in an intellectual way. This is not what the Master Jesus would have. The interpretation of this ancient truth, this profound and eternal truth, which the Master brought to you, must be the interpretation of the spiritual power. It must not be just the letter, it must be the power of the spirit in human hearts.

The Master Jesus caused to be formed, while he was on earth among men and women, groups of brethren to whom he taught the esoteric truth. You have in the four gospels certain phrases which Jesus used which are pregnant with spiritual power and life, but they are reported parrot-fashion today, without any understanding of their spiritual force. This spiritual power can only come when the words are used with knowledge and with understanding of their true meaning. In the groups of brothers and sisters (because there were always sisters in these groups), the Master Jesus gave the key which enabled the aspirant to unlock the gates of heaven, the gates of that great world of life and light and power.

You have the key now, but forgive us for saying that many people are lethargic. With their minds they want to understand and prove all things, but they do not all take into account the life which is planted in the heart chakra. Within your innermost mind lies this power. The groups were taught by the Master and the other brethren of the ancient order how to tap into this magical power and release it in themselves, and apply it to life on the outer, material plane.

When you read the words in the Bible which the Master Jesus spoke, such as 'I AM the way and the truth and the life' and 'I AM the resurrection and the life', remember that he was conveying to his listeners that the life within him was the divine power itself. If only brothers and sisters would live by that inner power! It is the light which lights every man and woman on the path to the kingdom of heaven.

When Jesus said these words, he was endeavouring to convey to the little circle of his own days that within them God had planted this little light. Live by that light and it will bring to you love and life and power. You let trivial things absorb you instead of going right to the Father and saying: 'Father, Thou knowest my need; Father, work through me, let Thy power flow through me'. You would find that the power within you would work like magic, and instead of being strained and weary you would be buoyant and light and joyous, and you would be filled with this power of life.

You should not feel weary in body or mind if you endeavour to realize this glorious light and presence which is within you always, and to feel the presence of those brothers and sisters of the light who are all around you – and are very sorry when they see that you are allowing yourselves to become overburdened by those things which are unnecessary.

The Master Jesus instructed the inner groups he formed how to pray, how to meditate, how to live. He demonstrated many, many times to these inner groups the power of God. He healed the sick, he raised the dead (so-called), he walked on the water; he performed many miracles, all of them demonstrating that the power of God worked through him. But *What I do, shall ye do also* ... it is the simple law, the divine law that operates through matter in all forms.

Test our words for yourselves: test them, my children, now. As you sit quietly, use the phrases: 'I AM the way.... I AM the resurrection and the life...'. Feel that power rising in you, your whole body aglow, vibrating with this spiritual life. It is eternal life, and this is what Jesus was endeavouring to teach the world. He, and many others in the ancient past, taught the people the same secret.

You must act; God must be brought through you, God in action in your life ... and all the love of the Brotherhood behind the veil is with you in that power of God.

What does it matter if you gain the whole world materially if you lose your soul – if you lose this divine power, this love of God from your hearts? Then you will be dead. The life of the spirit slowly dies in the materialist, and the body becomes heavy and dull and diseased; but the body of the spiritually alive becomes light and alive and quick; it becomes on fire with the divine life. The healing power is the Christ power flowing through.

We follow the teaching about Jesus and his brethren with one about another great teacher whose example is immensely powerful in brotherhood, the one known as the Lord Buddha — and with a short passage about the coming together of East and West, which seems to be happening at the present time as brotherhood grows naturally on earth.

May all brethren feel the compassion of Buddha, the peace of his soul and the wisdom which lies in his stillness and his love ... the glorious compassion which flows from his heart. His humility and his gentleness, his earthly poverty, his renunciation and his devoted service both to the animal kingdom and the human has caused the world to turn to the East in worship and thanksgiving for his life, his teaching and the extraordinary power which he still exerts on earth.

This Buddhic power is of the utmost importance and necessity, particularly to the western world. The activity of the mind, the rapid progress of the mental body, and the rapid increase of materialism in the West, all call for the permeation of the rays from the heart of the Lord Buddha into the hearts of western people.

We view this spiritual force with great respect and thankfulness, and we do not see it only in its effect upon the lower plane of life; we see also its effect from above. We see the distribution of the rays of peace and power. We see the influence of the Lord Buddha very much upon the world today, and particularly upon young people. If you will observe their reactions, their tastes, their aspirations, you will notice for instance how readily they turn away from cruelty to the animal kingdom. The more advanced souls who are in the bodies of children have brought with them the influence of the Lord Buddha. We are speaking, of course, of the enlightened ones. They are coming now into bodies already enlightened by this buddhic influence.

But what happens? As soon as they come into family life, school life and, later on, business life (or whatever their form of service to humanity), they meet a wall of materiality – and their chakras, which were by then gently opening through the soul influence of the past life, shut down; and the responsibility for this closing down of these windows of the soul rests upon the older generation on earth. It is necessary then for brethren like ourselves – we speak from the spirit world but we are one with you – to listen patiently and to guide wisely the young, along the path of enlightenment. We must not be intimidated by the worldliness of the world! We must be simple and true to the inner light in our relationship with our children, the future generation.

You will witness the light of the Sun rising in the East and travelling to the West, and there will come upon earth the unification of the teachings of the East with the application of that teaching in the West.

The passivity of the eastern mind will be translated into the action of the western mind, and there will come upon the earth this marriage, the unification of the two. There shall be born therefrom the perfect man–woman upon earth: born without desire, but through the divine will and by the sacred word. In your daily life, work unceasingly for humanity and the transmutation of the lower self into the divine, into the God being. Peace be in your souls.

With a slight change of tone, the next passages contain further teaching about the power of the light, and begin to show us what the manifestation of the light actually means in the context of how we are with one another. The qualities of brotherhood start to develop in us as we open receptively to the spiritual sunlight.

The ancient brethren knew that the spiritual forces surrounding the earth keep up the evolution of cycle upon cycle of life, breathed forth from the heart of God. O beloved brethren of today, take this same light with you! Let the spiritual forces abide in your hearts and radiate from your lives!

It is easy to be cheerful when there is something on the outer plane to be cheerful about, but not so easy when the earth is shrouded in darkness – but it is at these times that your test comes. It is easy to be kind when everyone is kind, easy to be loving when others are loving. But there is no credit in that. The

43

wise brother or sister knows that the light is always shining in the heavens; that it is only a question of a little time. Sense of the limitation of time brings all the confusion and heartaches to humanity. Time is the great limiter, but it is the great healer, and in God's time, you see the wisdom working behind the shadows. But you are inclined to forget, when the shadows are dense, that God's wisdom is at work. We know (and you know, when you raise your consciousness above the clouds) that the sun is shining and that the life of Christ is the only enduring life. That which is not of Christ must disintegrate, because it lacks the force which holds life on its course.

It is the love vibration that holds all things in place. Think of this. Love is ever constructive, ever progressive; therefore, think in terms of God's love. In the world today chaos exists, but behind this chaos is the power of love, and the brotherhood of men and women is a reality. Put aside all the manifestations apparent to you in the world and see, behind life, brotherhood. By thinking thus you hasten the time forward when that brotherhood will be manifested in the outermost circle of life.

As we come among you, we rejoice in your love. It is difficult for some of you to detach yourself from the idea of personal love. If your love is limited by the personal, that is alright, for it is at the moment the love that you understand. Love is born in the heart

44

as love for anther person. We learn through personal love, but beyond this there must grow the love of God, or the love for that which is good, wholesome, or holy. 'Holy' means healthy, wholesome. So love which is healthy and wholesome grows in our hearts, and we find ourselves loving life, which is holy, or healthy and wholesome, which is constructive, progressive, and is growing healthily towards perfection.

Bear patiently the difficulties and the problems of the present time, but know that God, all love and all wisdom, holds humanity in His–Her clasp. Right will conquer, and justice will balance apparent wrongs. God is no respecter of the wishes of persons or nations, and knows only justice; but at the same time brings to bear, on human affairs, love, healing and peace.

Another important lesson will then be learnt ... of the tenderness and the wisdom and the love of God. You must all have experienced it at some time or another in your own lives. Remember, then, that all is well. Control your hastes; be patient, all is well....

If you would be happy, my brothers and my sisters, and give happiness to all you contact, seek the quiet places of the spirit, and discriminate between the unreal, which is of the world, and the reality, which is of the spirit. Watch quietly, in confidence; never let your confidence be shaken, but watch confidently the gradual breaking through of this light in the affairs of the world. The dawn of this glorious brotherhood is now appearing.

We close this chapter with a selection of sayings about brotherhood, in each of which White Eagle's smiling countenance seems to manifest. Face to face with his own disciples, he says only a handful of devoted souls are needed to bring forward the rest: this applies in separate contexts all round the world.

If you will endeavour to become a channel for the love of God, or the Christ love for humanity, you will find it easier to work from the heart. When you are told to send forth a ray of light to darkened, suffering humanity, try to fill your heart with compassionate love, sympathy and pity for all who are unhappy and tortured in mind or in body. Then you will be a channel for an outpouring of love, and it will find the level of human need and receptivity.

Remember you are as a broadcasting station; your human vibration is used by the Wise Ones, by our Elder Brethren, to step down the waves of love to human need. You are individually used as you mix with the outer world. Will you remember when you are in the outer world, and among your brethren on the earth plane, to preserve in your heart the strength of the spirit of Christ; the strength of knowledge that all is working together for the good of humanity? Give forth good thought — love

46

thought. Move about among men and women as a power of peace and love.

God needs only a handful of true and worthy sons and daughters, and then can use them to bring peace among humankind. Peace on earth, and goodwill … to all.

*

Love; love much. Love each other, love all nature, love your brethren of the animal kingdom. Reach out through the dark veil of illusion, the dark veil of matter, into that higher mental world, to the brotherhood of the nature spirits, the brotherhood of angels and the brotherhood of the great solar universe. You are in *it*.

*

Do not many people believe that pain and suffering are humanity's inheritance? We prefer to look upon the other side of things. We are convinced that God created humanity to be happy. Happiness is your goal, my brethren, not misery, not suffering. Happiness must necessarily be shared. Human beings cannot be happy all to themselves; to be wholly happy, you must be sharing heaven. And so the purpose of all the teaching that comes to us from the White Brotherhood above is to point the way to happiness. Most surely if we have strength, or if we pray steadfastly to our Father–Mother God for strength, we shall attain happiness; and more, not only shall we

47

attain happiness ourselves, but we shall bring many souls along the path to happiness.

*

We work with you to raise the vibrations of your physical life, your physical body. We serve you in this way when we endeavour to bring you the spiritual realization of the true life of the spirit. And do bear in mind, wherever you are, wherever you go on this earth planet, that you are bearers of the light. You are pioneers of the new dispensation: you are light-bearers. You cannot leave where you are and go out into the world without taking with you the power, the light which will illumine the earth and the soul of humanity.

Your true destiny is to be pioneers for the life of the spirit, the life of the Great White Light. We repeat that you are light bearers. This means that you live in consciousness of the light: you realize that your body is light, that everything around you is light. Dwell in the light. Imagine that you are a body of light, a cross radiating the colours of the spectrum and colours that are unknown in your spectrum: magnificent and radiant colours that are unknown from your sun. If you live in the consciousness of your true nature, you will indeed carry the light.... Keep on, light bearers ... light bearers, brothers of the Great White Light, the Circle of the Christ!

48

A Prayer to the Father

O beloved Father God, Who art the life and the light of all creation, we Thy children would raise ourselves unto Thee. We would know and see the living truth and the light; and would become united with Thee in perfect life and glory, and draw all beings – our brethren! – into Thy light and Thy healing and Thy perfection.

O Father God, may Thy children see, through love, the life of all dear to them; the life of all creation of every kingdom on earth, enfolded in Thine ineffable sweetness and peace. Thus, O Father God, shall the fret and strain of the false life fall away, and they enter into the fulness of Thy kingdom. Thus may their sorrow be turned to happiness; thus may there be no weeping and no night, but for all the day of joy and life eternal.

CHAPTER 3

Brotherhood in the Spirit

In this chapter, White Eagle firmly sets out a vision of the brotherhood in spirit, showing how it is the model for the brotherhood we seek to create on earth. Through recognizing it as central to the divine plan, we learn about its gentle coming to earth.

In the first extracts, we explore a sense of spirit — and earth — as one united whole, existing both sides of the veil between life and so-called death. White Eagle describes how we may discover our spirit helpers and work with them. It is a grand scheme that he offers as our future.

THE WORLD is advancing. In the world each one of you is needed; each one is a spoke in the wheel, and we bless you, all brethren, for we work together to bring light, knowledge, wisdom, love, into the hearts of all peoples. When these groups of White Brethren are formed all over the world, as they will be, the light will perform spiritual miracles in physical matter and the governments will all unite in service.

The time is not distant when the White Brotherhood will be the established religion of all peoples. Materialism will die, through the spirit rising like a fire in the heart of man and woman. This is the way of evolution. The pure white light is like a white fire which cannot be extinguished. People may try to smother it, as they do at the present time, but the flames of truth will burst forth. We only need to let the divine fire burn brightly upon our own altar, the one within the temple of our own soul, and we shall set free many another soul.

So, my brethren, in the words used in the ancient days of Atlantis, we say: 'Let the light shine! Let the divine fires burn upon the sacred altar'.

*

Your work means continually remembering the spiritual state of life from which your spirit has come and to which it will return. It means continually making an effort to live with the spiritual values ever in your heart and mind, to live refusing to be entangled or held down by wrong values; and when you see the right, keep to the right and do not be influenced by material conditions. The spiritual law is such that it will never lead you astray. If you follow the truly spiritual law you cannot go wrong, but you will have to have the courage to hold fast to a decision in favour of spiritual law.

This will help you to keep your contact with the White Brotherhood in the world of spirit. By this we do not mean only the exalted beings, but all those kindly, sincere, loving friends who are yours on the spirit planes of life. Do you know, my sisters and brothers, that many of these friends are around you now, acting as silent helpers, silent watchers ever on the lookout for opportunities to serve and to help, to guide and to inspire you? These more lowly brethren are yet pure in heart; although they may not have attained a high degree of spiritual knowledge, save only simple wisdom and love, they stand as keepers of the door between you and the heavens. They would help you to open that door. So we urge you to be true in your friendship and your love for these silent helpers. If the light of the Star shines from your heart, you have no need to fear any contact with the world of spirit; and through this doorway into the realms of light and truth you will pass to make contact with greater beings.

The simplest way, possibly, to arrive at a consciousness of brotherhood both sides of the veil is to expand our awareness of brotherhood on the earth plane, and see it reaching out from the merely human world to include the whole of life — meaning not just other creatures but the entire organism of earth, and even the other planets and stars.

For more on the Great Mother of all life, see chapters seven and eight below, especially pp. 148-50, 164, 183-4. All creation is simplified to one common denominator — love. When you can go into the fields and the woods, and feel the common brotherhood of the trees and grass and wind and sky, the birds and animals; when you can feel as one, and realize there is no separation, and you touch the heart of creation, which is love ... then you have looked into the heart of God.

You cannot go wrong if you think always of love towards your brothers and sisters on earth and towards all creation. Love the animals, the birds, the fish in the sea, and the flowers that bloom and give perfume for your delight and joy; love the trees which give shade and all lovely things in colour and form and music. Love all, for all are created by love and there is nothing that God has ever hated, no single thing. What is regarded as evil has its work to do in bringing forth light out of its own darkness.

Be at peace, then, for your mission is to *be* peace; and your mission is to be constructive in your thought, not destructive. We reiterate that the world is moving forward towards one great brotherhood of life. Let us all remember once again that we are one with all life, that there is the one lifestream running through every form of life on many planes of consciousness. And we are part of this grand universal lifebeat. By loving life, and loving our brethren, we are putting all our strength into the Great White Light which slowly but surely is dominating humanity.

Light *is* love. The law of the White Brotherhood is love to all creation, and service springing from the heart. The rule of the White Brotherhood is unity of spirit, at-one-ment. After you have made your commitment, anything in your life which violates this spiritual law will place you outside the Brotherhood. Your own action will do this. It is your privilege to serve with all your soul your suffering brethren on earth, to bring light in the darkness, and peace and goodwill to all people. If sorrow comes to you, remember always your beloved Father in heaven Who leads you, His child, into green pastures, and by the still waters of the spirit.

You have also heard, on many occasions when we have spoken, references to the gentle Mother. Again the message is that you work in co-operation with this spirit of wisdom and love which is the Mother of the Christ Child. The Mother is the heavenly and cosmic power that is the source of the life and the truth and the love, which in turn is the salvation of humankind. It is no use for wars to cease on the outer plane without a corresponding cessation of war between the light and the dark forces on the inner planes. And so your work must go on and on. May all brothers and sisters bear with them into the world the spirit of the holy gentle Mother who will give birth to the Christ on earth.

Commune all day with those companions of the spirit who now walk their way rejoicing in the light and love of their Master, the Christ. May his love sing, sing in your hearts and minds.

White Eagle's own role is not always understood: as we have seen, he generally describes himself simply as a 'spokesman' for the Brotherhood in spirit. Here he speaks of those with whom he works. In the first extract, the concept of masters is introduced and is one we shall explore later in the chapter (pp. 61–3).

Beloved brethren, we are the messengers from the Great White Brotherhood, who send you all love, all love and peace, peace. The White Brethren live to serve God and humanity. They work continuously in the remote mountain levels, meditating and concentrating and strengthening their consciousness of God and sending to humanity the light and power which swells and radiates from them as a brotherhood. And they would have you individually know that you may receive the strength of their love. Whatever your need, whether it arise from sickness, or loneliness, or anxiety, if you will remember to look towards them you will receive immediate help, power and peace, and a sense of well-being.

Wherever there is a responsive heart, and a responsive personality, the masters redouble their efforts upon that one. We would have you all know of the greatness of this unknown brotherhood of the spirit which is working now through humankind. It is working particularly through those who, like yourselves, are responsive to mental impressions – for remember, spirit works through mind. It is working through those of you who are responsive to the spirit, so that you may be great. When we say great we do not mean known on earth, we mean noble in spirit, allowing the divine power to work in you and radiate from you for the upliftment and blessing of your fellow creatures on earth. So we join with you and with all initiated sisters and brothers throughout the world in thanking all those in higher spheres who have helped humankind to receive this divine truth that life is spirit.

All round you are beautiful beings, though you cannot see them unless you are very elevated in consciousness, and then you can become attuned to the plane of life in which these beings live. We can only tell you that there are these beings; and indeed, as we talk to you, behind us is a group of very much greater beings than ourselves, and behind that group is an even more advanced group – and so on, right through the spiritual spheres.

You do not begin to comprehend the invisible beings who are working with humanity. You do not yet glimpse the great powers that you have within you and that are within these higher ethers. Just a little demonstration has come through to you in suitable places, but we do assure you that men and women of science in the higher worlds are working in suitable groups and with certain human brains which can receive knowledge from guides and teachers which will be of inestimable value to human life in future.

As we speak we have before us a vision of the beautiful light which is the divine essence of love. You may be conscious of your physical life and the physical room, but to us these things are only illusion, and what you and we really behold is a temple built of shining white substance, through which are passing all the colours of the spectrum. This temple is the Star Temple, the universal temple; it is our habitation, dear brethren, whenever we come specially into the service of the Christ Brotherhood. This temple is eternal and universal, infinite. It is nothing new; and it is from this temple in the heavens that all through the ages humanity has drawn its inspiration. Let us remember that the servers in this temple are always 'about their Father's business'. They never weary of service; indeed, the joy of their life, of their very existence, is in the service of the Son of God. It is the oldest and the simplest truth known to humanity.

White Eagle now speaks of the antiquity of the brotherhood, the moment when the great truth of life came from spirit into earthly form. In the first passage, he had first led his listeners into meditation.

You have raised your hearts to the White Lodge above, where dwell the elder brethren. You are not separated from your elder brethren, unless you separate yourself from the brotherhood of life by doubt and fear and disharmony; but you draw near to your elder brethren through gentleness and peace within your soul, and love towards all living creatures. We are very close to you, dear brethren, but while you live in the flesh, the veil of dense matter will normally separate you from the brotherhood invisible. As you serve with unflinching courage and strong faith in the powers invisible, you will in time find the veil which hangs between your world and ours dissolve.

Now, dear ones, as you come deeper into meditation you are *en rapport* with the Great White Brotherhood. You hear so much about the White Brotherhood, but you do not fully understand what this brotherhood is. Imagine that you are in the presence of ancient Wise Ones – not beings of your present world cycles, but great souls of all time. Oh yes! – for as the soul grows in God-consciousness and in spirituality, it grows in stature also. These great spiritual intelligences are great in form and beauty; and there are many whom you would not recognize as human beings or as people who have been human beings.

Listen, for you are in the company, on the inner planes, not only of those dear ones whom you have known all through your history and even in your present incarnation, but with those beings who peopled the earth millions of years ago. Moreover, you are not only in contact with ageless souls who were once human beings, but you are also in the company of beings who dwell on other planets. This is important for you to know, and all that we tell you is important for you to know and for you to believe and to realize, because progress is now rapid on your earth plane and humans have to become much more spiritualized to enable them to attract and to converse with beings from other planets.

The plan, the ideal, was given to men and women of ages and ages past. Through human beings it came, beings whom your very clever people once used to call savages! It is well to remember that a body which appears to be savage is the remnant of a great being. We are referring particularly to an ancient race that we will call an Indian race, an Indian of the West not the East. You have no conception at all of the age of our Indian brotherhood.

Oh dear, how do you think the Indian received his crown of feathers? The more modern Indian wears his feathers or later on receives the crown of the chief – called, in more degenerate times, the war bonnet. Yet every feather in that chief's headdress signifies something, a test overcome, a quality developed, a great deed performed. Every feather was significant. In your modern days you talk of 'a feather in your cap', little knowing the basic truth of that idea or where it came from. We hope you will remember that as you pass your tests or do a brave deed or a loving deed, you receive a feather in your cap. We may sound facetious, but on the contrary we are very serious.

You may remember the story given through our channel Minesta of the Plumed Serpents in the Americas.*You have no one on the earth at the present time like them, for they come of a very ancient race which was most highly developed. They came into incarnation on the earth plane to teach the human race and to establish an ideal, the ideal of brotherhood and peace among the nations.

It is true that all down the ages messengers have come to humanity, culminating in that great elder brother and Master, Jesus. Together with all the Christian love and the peace of the Buddha and the love of all the saints, the great and goodly company, any little brotherhood you may be part of today originated from that ancient Indian brotherhood who lived in a land which is now completely under the sea. Yet the remains of that brotherhood was also established in the secret places of the Andes and the Himalayas.

The Plumed Serpents wore their crowns of plumes – which were really emanations, radiations of the beautiful aura which was theirs. The plumed feather emanations were only radiated by very advanced beings whom you could not comprehend

*It is recounted in most detail in Grace Cooke's MEMORIES OF REINCARNATION (Liss, Hants., 2006)

today. The ancient truths we offer you are on the innermost planes, and it is only when you have learnt how to reach those innermost planes that you will be rewarded with the wisdom and the power and the love, the sweetness of spirit which your brethren of ancient days used in the service of all creatures.

There is a connection between the ones White Eagle calls the Plumed Serpents and the more 'western' concept of the beings known as the masters. White Eagle speaks of them separately, but in the main he plays down any concept of individual identity when he calls on such groups of Wise Ones: not through this implying that they cannot be distinct so much as that being united in purpose and service, these Beings only need individuality so that they may be recognized on earth, not because they need it in spirit. Through long experience they have risen above earthly illusions of separation.

Many of you think with love and worship of the masters. The term 'master' means one entered into the cosmic and universal consciousness and who has attained spiritual mastery over the physical life. For this reason, in attaining mastership the masters have overcome death, and are untouched by the decay of physical matter. The masters are very beautiful brothers and sisters worthy of your love and your reverence, but they have had to travel the same path as you are now journeying, and have had to learn in the same way to master the lower self, to master all physical conditions, physical atoms; and the way to this is continual, almost constant, communion and prayer. Even when you are out in the world remember that over the heads of the throng you can see the face of the Master, if you look. Seek this Presence always in your life and you shall find God, and in the finding will come to you mastery of yourself.

There are masters and elder brethren unknown to humanity all over the world. They make no claims: their work is chiefly on the inner planes, and they are working behind all human beings and influencing the leaders of humanity. They work silently and invisibly. They give their help to certain groups and religious organizations and to all the good things that are born on earth. All the groups which are born with the ideal of service and brotherhood have behind them one or perhaps two or even sometimes three of the elder brethren who will lend power and guidance and help to that group.

The masters of the White Brotherhood are universal in their service; they are behind all institutions working for humankind. There are centres or lodges in which these brethren meet on the earth plane, but they are in remote places passed by by the outside world – which is not allowed to intrude upon the sanctuaries of the brotherhood. There are lodges in the Andes, in the Himalaya, in Egypt, in

62

the northern and southern regions. All over the world are these lodges where the elder brethren meet and from which they direct their power and light to humankind....

*

Beloved brethren, we would take you in spirit to the mountains in the East, to the centre or the city of light, and would open your vision and your consciousness to a spiritual ceremony which is taking place. Do not think only with your earthly minds; go deep, deep into the realms of spirit and you will find yourselves in the vast temple of the ancient wisdom, where there are assembled many great beings, including planetary beings and messengers from the spiritual sphere of life, from an invisible planet. Meditate on them.

Although there is more about earthly brotherhood in the next chapter, some of White Eagle's teaching helping us to link our earthly experience with the brotherhood in the heavens may be useful here.

No man or woman can lead or help others that has not attained a degree of self-mastery. Self-mastery means letting the God power so control the lower earthly nature that the glorious Christ light, the spirit of the beautiful Christ, will operate through you to the glory of the Father–Mother: your Father, your Mother, God, the first two principles of life.

What we tell you is in accord with science: physical and spiritual science.

You are told that through the Star* you are linked with the Master. This is absolutely true, but we should like to broaden your conception of the Master. The Master is not one limited personality, the Master is unlimited. Shall we say it is divine intelligence which uses the individual brother or sister, whoever and whatever he or she is? When you are brought *en rapport* with this life you are instantly used by that spiritual life-force, and it cannot miss because you have created in your soul the attraction which draws it to you.

We want you to understand that when you work together to send out the light, not only is the concentration of your own thought going forth from the centre on earth where you work, but actually surrounding such a group is a host of unseen witnesses. We want you to know that behind you and around you there are countless white-robed brethren. The white robe is actually the aura of those brethren. It is the pure white raiment or clothing of the spirit, and as you work you too are weaving about yourselves the same pure white raiment as you learn to contact the Christ within your soul.

There is a divine plan on the table in the council chamber of the masters of humanity; but human-

*See chapter five.

64

kind is needed in order to carry out this plan. The masters can only build to this plan with the aid of the builders on the earth. Those who work with the light are the builders of the future. You are the pioneers and you are at present laying the foundation for a new humanity; but the progress of this building depends upon the individual worker and the life and the thoughts and the vision of the individual brother or sister. It sounds very grand, but it *is* grand. The plan is for the spiritualization and the beautification of the life of man and woman, first of all on this planet. But there is no limit to the progress and the glory of the spirit, because you are of the same spirit as the Creator.

It would not do for you to have your eyes fully opened to the radiance of the spiritual beings who work with humanity – you could not stand to live in your earthly life if you felt too powerfully the vibrations of these godlike brethren. But we would convey to you occasionally a picture of their radiance and love. You talk of love and aspire to love – you do so valiantly in your service – but even so, you cannot yet comprehend the beauty of these angelic ministers.

In spirit there is no separation; you are not shut away from this glorious brotherhood we describe to you – only insofar as you shut yourself away. You as an individual can close around you a barrier of despair and darkness and fear, and then you separate yourself from this brotherhood, for they cannot break through your reserve: it is all against the law. The brotherhood will never intrude, but if you open your heart and say, 'come', they come, so joyously, and will never fail.

In the passages that follow White Eagle describes a little how the impulse from spirit enters and develops our consciousness, so that we are guided, not working at random. This section takes up from one in the first chapter (pp. 17–19) on the power of thought and also explains how we can be of healing service to those around us.

O beloved brethren, the love there is for humanity among those who are in the Grand Lodge above! — the yearning, love and desire to help their brethren, to save humanity from the sufferings of the lower self. It is only through thought power and love power that humanity can be touched and helped and guided. Some find it difficult to understand the methods employed by those in the spirit life, but you will come to see on your earth that only by thoughts of a constructive nature can you help those who are unhappy and who suffer. Once thought is planted as a seed in the minds of men and women, then action follows.

No action comes without thought. Thought is of primary importance in the healing of wounds, in the restoration of peace, and in the power of reconstruction. And this applies to health, to spiritual progress, and unfoldment, and to material needs. Let God be in your heart and in your understanding, and you will find that nothing is wanting in your life. Be not impatient or anxious. The light will bring forth into manifestation on earth that which is good for you in God's sight.

The power of the love thought can do anything. It is creative, it is indeed all-power. Everything is wrought by the power of thought and your work is one of learning to use the power of thought. You are just on the edge of the great discovery, but you have to use this power rightly. There must be no question of drawing anything to yourself by this power, but only a thought for the good of the greatest number. We, as individuals, are nothing, and yet, in another sense, we are everything when we have learnt to expand and radiate into the infinite. We seriously say to you that thought power is the mightiest power in life, and it is to be used for the good of all life. In the process of the individual working for the good of the whole, for the progress of the whole, it is inevitable that the individual is raised in the power of love into her own heaven and into his own good.

We return now to a more meditative awareness, in which White Eagle helps us make our own contact with the brethren above. In the final meditation (p. 70) White Eagle refers to the symbol of the Star, as he did a few sections back. The

Star and its meaning are described more fully in chapter five.

The veil of the temple being torn asunder is a reference to St Matthew 27:51.

Down through the ages groups of men and women have lived in communion with the angels and the brethren of the Great White Light. Such men and women have been drawn from all races ... and from all levels of society. They only recognize one truth, and that truth is God within them. They live under the direction of their inner light; they have always a ready ear for the guidance and ministration of those who come to them from the spirit world; for these White Brethren on earth walk hand in hand with the brethren in the spirit world, and their lives are interpenetrated by the spiritual power of the White Brethren in the spirit world.

Those radiant ones behind and above us seek channels through whom they can spread the light of Christ on earth. What is the light of Christ? We call it the Golden Rule: the rule of love, the doing unto others as you would like to be done unto. Not many understand the full implication of this Golden Rule, which must govern every detail of life. Through you the angels and the White Brothers work to spread this light, which is the teaching of the Golden Rule. You beloved earthly brethren have been presented with a great and beautiful gift of spiritual power and love in the form of your opportunity for service.

Many organized religions become as an empty shell and their people so enveloped in materialism that they are deaf and blind to the true spirit. But remember the true light of Christ, of love and gentleness, of humility and justice, is the same yesterday, today and for ever. It can never die. It is always with humanity. It is only that the individual human being does not recognize or allow it to express itself through his or her mind and speech and action. Masters, teachers, saviours of all time have given out the same teaching – because it is the jewel of great price.

The heavy veil of materialism which now hangs between the world and the spiritual life will be torn down. This is the rending of the veil in the holy temple of Christ, and it is the meaning of the words, 'The veil of the temple shall be torn asunder'. For men and women are the temple of God, their forms created in the image and likeness of God. That veil in the temple is of darkness, selfishness and materialism and hides from human beings their inner holy of holies. When the veil has been torn down every human will be guided by the light of God in his or her heart, and the Christ Light shall illumine the earth, and all people shall be blessed.

A Meditation on Brotherhood

Picture the assembly of all the White Brothers in the heavens. They are around you, come to serve you, to free you from imprisonment. They come to help you behold the kingdom of heaven and enter in. Rejoice with them for your creation.

Now, at this moment, we ask you to lay aside the activity of your brain and open your heart chakra. Expand your soul into the higher white ether. You can do this by steadily and steadfastly creating an image of the spirit Brotherhood as we shall describe it to you. We would remind you that when we speak of brotherhood we mean not just a collection of people, but an awareness, a realization in your soul of the at-one-ment of life. In order to comprehend the meaning of brotherhood and to realize it in your soul and heart, you must rise above the physical level of consciousness.

When you are working on the physical level and your brain becomes active, many queries arise as to what brotherhood is, and you are held down and buried in the dust of earth, and there you are blinded by the human attributes, the failings of humankind. So we raise you in consciousness, in thought and imagination, into the temple of the Great White Brotherhood in the white ether, far removed from the darkness of physical life and physical matter. As we enter the temple of the White Brotherhood we are instantly aware of stillness, peace and radiance: a radiation of the divine essence of love. Let us dwell in the brotherhood community now and feel the unity, the love which all of these brethren have for you, for all humankind, for all creation.

The Brotherhood of the Light is very, very aware of the efforts of humanity to establish justice on the earth, and they work as you are working to project the Star symbol over the earth. We wish that our brethren would more frequently use the symbol of the Star. Think of the Star, remember that you are the Star when you are perfectly balanced, for the Star is the symbol of the Christ being, man–woman made perfect, the one on earth completely balanced, with attention to the material and physical needs of life, not his or her own life but life as a whole on the earth planet.

And being aware of the need of life you aspire, you open your heart and your consciousness to love, for you learn that love is the great healer. You open your heart to Christ, for Christ is love. Christ is the power of love and the wisdom of love, and all souls who are aware of the spiritual rays and the cosmic rays of love are within the circle of the White Brotherhood. Because they are attuned to the Brotherhood of the Light they are in it. We hope that you can comprehend what we are endeavouring to teach you.

CHAPTER 4

A Brotherhood for You

White Eagle has been showing us how although we may aspire to create brotherhood between people and peoples, the model for brotherhood is fundamentally shown us once we learn to make contact with the world above us. In short, a developing sense of brotherhood is the coming to earth of love from above. This time we begin in a meditative space.

ON A MOUNTAINTOP is a quiet sanctuary, a place of meditation: a temple open at the sides. The roof appears to be open also, and yet there is a covering, a canopy, above. The brethren in that temple are kneeling in prayer, praying for their brethren below on earth. Behold! A white dove descends upon that kneeling group; a white dove of peace goes forth across the world with an olive branch in its beak.

These things are true. From this brotherhood a message was sent across the world to certain chosen people, directing them to gather together a group of loving men and women who were awakening to the spiritual forces of wisdom and love. This group was to be formed into a brotherhood. First, the men and women were to learn to practise brotherhood among themselves. They could not be perfect – this the Wise Ones knew – but they could have the aspiration towards true brotherhood, and therefore they would become channels through which the powers of this brotherhood on high could send light to the world. They could send a steadying, calming influence to humanity at a time of humanity's greatest need.

Much can be accomplished with faithful and true brethren. We offer you the calling to be a bearer of the light. For long ago it was foreseen that if a group of true Brothers in the light of Christ could stand together with courage and serenity of spirit, humanity could be saved without plunging too far into the depths of the years of fire that mark the passage from one age to the next.* And so we give unto you this charge – to take no thought for yourselves, but to labour ceaselessly for humanity.

Keep the serenity of the mountaintop, and of that quiet, still temple. When in the midst of the turmoil of human beings you feel shaken, and fear creeps in, then we bid you remember those white-robed figures in prayer ... and you will be restored.

Your work is clear. You are needed to succour, to comfort. Quietly, then, proceed with your work; quietly and serenely go forward. Be of good heart; your work is not in vain.

*That is, from the age of Pisces to that of Aquarius. This message dates from early in that transition.

73

After this very beautiful meditation, White Eagle offers a picture of our openness to receive the message of brotherhood. He briefly surveys what might be asked of us in the creation of brotherhood on earth.

At some time love comes to every human being. This means that each will be loved by someone, some-where, and each will unfold love within their own being. It does not matter on what plane such love manifests, because it comes according to the degree of the soul's awakening. No one can say, 'I have a greater degree of love than my brother or my sis-ter', for the lowliest soul can love. But the more awakened a soul, the more quickly does it recog-nize love in its simple and possibly crude form in its brother and sister. This is our work, brethren: to observe, understand and become unified with that love-quality which we should recognize instantly in the living soul of every one of our companions....

The light of the spirit can shine from your heart, from your whole body. There should be no separation between us and our sisters or brothers, no matter their class, creed, colour or race: we are all one. We must aspire to this realization of the uni-versal life.

*

You live not unto yourselves, but work for and serve the great world of spirit as well as the world of mat-ter. May this become an ever-increasing realization!

74

Each day and night* you send out rays of either harmony or discord — your contribution to the upliftment and peace (or otherwise) of millions of souls — for your vibrations touch the discarnate, and the vibrations of the discarnate reflect back upon the earth. Realize your responsibilities. Go about your daily life conscious always of unseen hosts looking to you, for the light of the White Brotherhood. Both love, and give.... Hold your brothers and sisters in this light, and there shall come peace on earth, 'goodwill towards men' — and women. You as an individual must realize your responsibility in this cause of universal love, wisdom and brotherhood.

One individual may lead a people; one soul may change the nations of the world. Let the light pour through you. Obey the Master — *love*.

*

There is no higher achievement, my brethren, than government of the self, mastery of the self. May the divine will within you, and which is sleeping within all men and women, rise and direct your lives ... the divine will which arises from the heart and gives, gives, *gives* goodwill to all creatures. We would like all

*White Eagle advocates a spiritual practice of some kind for everyone. In particular, he encourages those who follow his teachings to concentrate on the light of the sun or star and project that as a living force, wherever there is need. See also p. 115.

75

brethren to remember that all the good in the world springs from individual effort – first from the individual, then from the group, then from the nation; and thence comes one day the union of nations, with the people so represented that they govern themselves.

Having evoked a brotherhood on earth without boundaries or divisions and based on love, White Eagle begins to show us the possibilities of service that lie open to human beings. It may be work that we committed to in the past, and once we have committed, then we have engaged in a level of responsibility. But it is a joyous responsibility, not a heavy one. This passage closes with a meditational communion.

May every heart rejoice in the knowledge of the love which encompasses you, and may you use this knowledge to succour and bless your brethren on earth whom you daily serve.... You have felt the power of love which flows to humanity from the heart of your Creator. God works *through* humanity; God needs the co-operation of the *will* of humanity to enable his plan for spiritual evolution to progress. God needs His–Her children on earth to further this work of increasing love and brotherhood among men and women. Unless the human heart will open and respond to the gentle love of Christ, brotherhood and goodwill between you all cannot exist.

Many men and women now in incarnation can understand and respond to the truth and the spiritual application of the law of love. By working with the light you are among these; you have earned the privilege and opportunity of being shown how to broadcast, on the ether, rays of life and soundwaves of love to help humankind. These are mental wavelengths, more potent than material vibrations, and they are sent forth from your heart centre.

Strive then to project, with all the willpower in your heart, love and compassion to *all* people – not only to those whom you love. To send forth love to those you love has become a spontaneous reaction. You must hold in the will of your heart (not mind), love for all humanity. Love those whom the world calls your enemies, even those who seem to do great wrong. Do not fall into the error of regarding any other human being as your enemy. No man or woman is your enemy; they are your teachers, nationally as well as individually. Nations, and all men and women in the countries concerned, are being taught necessary lessons of brotherhood.

The birth pangs from which the earth is now suffering* are painful. The earth is labouring like a great animal giving birth to its young. We are now within a new cycle of life. The sun has entered Aquarius, and

*This passage and the next were both spoken in wartime, though there are plenty of 'birth pangs' remaining today. The reader interested in the Aquarian Age may be interested to consider White Eagle's book, THE LIGHT BRINGER, with its special focus on St John (for whom see also p. 23).

the age of Aquarius will continue – as far as Earth is concerned – for a whole cycle, roughly two thousand years. The symbol of the sign of Aquarius is the man carrying the water pot, and from this pot pours forth upon the earth the baptism and purification of the new spirit of brotherhood and goodwill. The age of Jesus was the age of Pisces.

The Master is now telling all brethren of the light to follow this Being of the new age, Aquarius, to the upper chamber (of the higher consciousness, the higher self) and make ready the communion table, and there partake – to drink and eat the wine and the bread of the spirit of Christ.

Partake! Hold this holy communion in your hearts, and become strong in Christ. Thus you will be at peace, raised above the worries of the material life. You will know that all that happens to you, your family, your business, your nation, is all in the plan for your good. You will have deep knowledge that if you walk steadily on your appointed path, all will be well; you will know that you are within the eternal heart of the Father–Mother God, and have nothing to fear.

Do not look upon the suffering of the body with too much emotion. God is all wisdom and has great love for those who suffer; all are protected and cared for by our loving Father, Whose love is infinitely greater than you can comprehend. There is hope! There is light! Welcome it with thankful hearts. All works for the good of all, but there are birth pangs, teething troubles and the falls and knocks of childhood which cannot be escaped. But all is well....

God be with you all. God be in your head and in your understanding. God be in your heart. God be with you in life, and in your passing through the gates and into the sunlit garden of your true home, the spirit world, the land of light.

By this point it should be clear that brotherhood is the pattern we are shown by spirit, and that it has a number of different aspects. One is a developing love for one another and for all life. Another is a closeness to spirit, which encourages and fires us in our work. But the aspect wherein we are totally counted upon by spirit is that of taking the radiant light that comes from the heart of being and using our own hearts to project it into the ignorance of matter, whether that means human beings tied to violence and conflict, cells of the body that can be healed by the inflow of light, or the agonies of a polluted planet. As we read, another purpose comes to the surface: that of bringing balance.

A question has been asked on the method of projecting light, on the method of giving sustenance to a particular person, place, ship....* Before commencing this work it is well to prepare for that

*White Eagle's instruction to his brethren in the wartime often included sending the light to a particular ship or point in the ocean, sometimes with great precision.

which is to follow; the object in the first place is to open the heart chakra, the one safe centre from which to work. We have already likened the heart centre to a fragrant rose. Lift your heart, not merely in lip service, but open your heart as a rose, hold it up as a rose to the sunlight. Remember that there are many planes between you and God, the Supreme, but there is a way which goes directly through all the planes of mind and emotion and astral desire. Open your heart directly to your higher self first, that part of you which functions above the limitations of the earth mind. You can reach your higher self through the heart centre – through love, humility and wisdom. Then you are prepared as a channel, and your prayer rises like the perfume of the rose.

You are a vessel to be filled with light, and in your great love for humanity you bring through images of the people you wish to help, of the place you wish to bless; there is no need for you to work hard, except to steady your mind and just bring through pictures, because that makes a point of focus. As soon as you bring the form through your mind you have focused it, and the light which is coming from the Most High, pouring into your heart, will go instantly – in a flash – to the person or place that you wish to help.

Your task is to be a peacemaker and a light-bearer. The Master says, 'Behold, I send you forth as peacemakers and light-bringers'. Radiate peace in your world and in your country. Do not allow yourselves to be pulled hither and thither by noisy talk; keep very calm and tranquil. Strive for inner strength and steadfastness.

We in the spirit rejoice in the progress, unseen by you, both mental and spiritual. Our work and yours is to bring balance to the massed thought of humankind, a balance between the mind and the spirit. There is a very rapid development of the mind, and the Brotherhood works to bring the light of heaven, the spiritual light, into this mind of man and woman – to hold the balance. This is of grave importance. The work of spiritually awakened and quickened souls is holding in balance the rapid mental development in humanity. Working from the heart centre not the mind, you wonder if you are doing any good. We have told you before, and we tell you again, and shall tell you many times, of the grave importance of the sending out of the light by the groups, brotherhoods who understand what they are doing. There are not too many who understand how to radiate that light. It is not just a form of prayer, it is an understanding of how to project the light into human life.

We have seen that brotherhood by White Eagle's definition is partnership, a partnership between workers on earth and workers in spirit. The need to develop a feeling of great harmony with and respect towards every other being is, as just stated, another aspect of brotherhood. The next passages remind us how important this is, and give a few words of encouragement. Some of the teaching that follows seems very much to relate to the small group White Eagle himself initiated; it is included as being an example of the relationship between each small group and the greater brotherhood in spirit.

All humanity is living eventually to realize its at-one-ment with love and with all humankind, with all life. Brotherhood is the goal, although you may not think so. Brotherhood is God, and when brotherhood is felt and realized and lived, then you have reached the highest consciousness humanity can reach. We bring love to you all individually – you who are our friends, brothers and sisters. We send to you now a wealth of love. We would like to bring to you a deeper feeling and comprehension of love, for this is what you are living for. We see you working in a very friendly spirit in the brotherhood you have created, and we watch over you with tender love.

It is only through human love and human relationships that you gradually rise and recognize at-one-ment with life and feel the truth of eternity, infinity, and the real meaning of brotherhood. When a brother can lose himself in service for others, or a sister have no more interest in the 'I' but only in 'we' and in 'all of us', then each has made a great advance on the path. Sometimes in meditation this indescribable at-one-ment, this heavenly light, is realized, until you become absorbed in it and there is no separation between you.

The work of the Brotherhood is not only to develop your own potential to send help to all humankind. You have to remember also that you have your own particular and private work to do in your own life, upon your own physical body, your own soul body and upon the expansion of your own God-consciousness. This means that, together with your selfless and faithful work in the group in which you work on the physical plane of life, you work upon yourself, in your own 'lodge', built round that divine spark deep within yourself.

You cannot hurry on your path: you have to learn first of all to harmonize with your fellow beings. You may not believe as they believe. They must follow their own urge. But you can believe that good is the ultimate outcome, that good comes in every situation. It does not matter what you have to endure. It does not matter what tests you go through. Remember that those tests are for your strength, your integrity, your understanding of the meaning of brotherhood. Remember this, and that you cannot hurry God. It is no use, my dear ones, trying to do this, because you will only tumble over big stones if you do! Have confidence that your heavenly Father—

ws when you are ready, and when you
e gates will open.

at sounds very simple, but if you meditate on · · words and think well on what we have
said, the meaning will be made ever plainer. 'The
gate will open.' This does not mean the gate between
life and death; it does not mean the gate between the
earth and the spirit world. It means that the gate of
the spirit will open, and you will advance into the
infinite garden of peace – of active peace. In turn
this means that you will thenceforth act with peace
in your heart.

To those of you who have been given the opportunity to lead a group or to serve in a group, remember
that the very first step is to create harmony. Always
work for harmony. It is more important than anything
else. Give way on little things which are not important, but be very strong and true on spiritual principles. Do not compromise between right and wrong.

The Master would say to you: 'Well done, your
work is good, you make excellent progress; but remember your feet are only on the first rung of a long
ladder. As you traverse that ladder, angels come from
heavenly places to accompany you upward to the
throne of God, into the company of the Sons of God
and of the attending angels of the Solar Logos....'

And so, beloved brethren, we leave you now,
touching each one with love....

Brotherhood holds no favourites, no prejudices, is unattached to earthly opinion. This does not mean that it cannot be accompanied by service through action upon the earth — far from it. But when it comes to political controversy, then White Eagle advocates remaining silent, but inwardly true.

In the next passages, he refers to the brotherhood on earth and in spirit as the Star Brotherhood — a term we shall come to understand better in the chapter that follows this.

The quotations are from St John, chapter 14, and St Matthew, chapter 6.

Remember that to do the work that you can do (or for any man or woman to do the work which he or she aspires to) you must be true and strong, not only in faith but in realization of the great power which is held by the Star Brotherhood in spirit. It is not a matter of talking, in fact the less you talk the greater and the stronger will be your spiritual power to serve, to comfort, to inspire, to heal your brethren.

We do not encourage taking sides within any controversy or having very strong opinions. We encourage you to seek the one true light, which is the Christ spirit, Christ the son of God. If you encourage his spirit, or the spirit of the Son within you, you are opening up these powers. The Master Jesus, the Christ, referred to that when he said of his miracles that when you work with the will of God, your Father, you will do these things as he does them, and

85

more besides. *Greater works than these shall [ye] do.* All through the ages the brotherhoods have been taught this secret. It is known as the white magic, but you must search for it and work for it.

Our work in the Brotherhood is to radiate the Christ spirit. We do not allow human opinions to creep in. The whole object of the work of this inner Brotherhood to which we belong is to increase the light of Christ in human conception, human understanding. If you allow political bias to creep in you are then opening yourself to the forces of chaos and darkness and confusion. You must be one-pointed and very clear in your work.

The light of the Son of God, all wisdom and all love, enfolds the whole of humankind – irrespective of class, race or creed. Above all things, you must be brethren of the Star and see to it that in your daily life you remain above the prejudices of race, class, creed or political opinion. Work for the Christ light.

Your work for brotherhood has to become more real to you than physical life itself. It is the light and the life and the power by which you live and move and have your being; and this you must realize more and more, and you will only realize it as you live in accordance with its law, the law so clearly and beautifully given in the words of the Lord Jesus Christ: *Seek ye first the kingdom of God ... and all these things shall be added unto you.*

86

You don't want to worry about what to do on earth, whether to write this letter or not, whether to do this or that. You don't want to worry about details. If you get the centre right everything around it will right itself. This is the lesson which has to be learnt before you can conquer the conditions of earthly life.

Finally, the reward of brotherhood is the experience of brotherhood itself: an awareness of our absolute indivisibility from all living things. Truly, all that we love is part of us; all that we might reach out to is already here, alive in the heart that is open to love. The section that follows is really about transformation, and the final remark is not to be taken out of context, but as a summary of all that has been presented so far. Understood thus, it will be recognized as one of the greatest aims any human being may have.

Brethren, you will find that all that lives in the eternal is the spirit, the higher truth, wisdom, power – all simplified into one attribute, one central ray: love.... We would teach you of the interpenetration of all spheres of life by one central power, love. You may, for instance, send your thoughts to the astral planes where there is disquiet: if you could only see the work you are doing! But you have to be content to work quietly, on the unseen planes. Nonetheless you are sending forth, by your love, rays of light, warmth, peace. As you do your attunement you experience a very beautiful, uplifting feeling. You feel, 'O Lord, it is good to be here!'

Live to love, love to live, thinking not of self, thinking only of the Great Self, which is universal brotherhood. Initiation into the mysteries of the spirit will first bring to you the consciousness of your at-one-ment with every form of life. The expansion of consciousness which comes with initiation into the White Lodge above brings love, universal love, without limitation. You just know that you are part of all life.

But what is this thing, this power, this joy which fills me thus? Oh . . . it is *good*, it is good. Why has it come to me? Because I have lost myself, my lower self. *My lower self has died, and all that remains is this joy, this love . . . for all people are my brethren. O God! I am Thy child. . . .*

*

If you open yourselves to the brotherhood influence, you will find that any physical sense of coldness will be changed into a warmth: the light in your own breast. Because you remain conscious of your physical body you feel its influence as cold. But if you let yourselves go into the light of the Spirit, and the power of the heavens, you will feel the warmth like a glowing fire in your heart. This is the source of all physical healing. This is the Great White Light that was used in the temples of the holy mysteries to heal the physical bodies of women and men. This Great White Light is the secret of creation, the power which alone can control and overcome all evil on earth.

This is why the light should always be used. Always look to the light, always absorb the light, and always give forth, in your thoughts, light. Commence with your own loved ones, and then extend your giving to all humanity and to all nature, to animals and birds and all forms of life. Send forth the light and warmth from the sacred fires of creation placed in your own being, and which can rise to your heart and head. Even in giving your hand in friendship, give forth through your hand the warmth of the Divine Fire.

We begin to feel the great fellowship of life, the infinite brotherhood of human beings with flower and tree, with wind and rain, with beast and bird, with all creation. This teaching brings to us the ever-widening realization that no one can live unto him- or herself and grow in happiness, no country live unto itself and prosper; there can be no progress without brotherhood, co-operation, unification. What we are telling you is scientific fact: the heart of each human being is beginning to take precedence over that which for centuries has been rising and threatening to overwhelm and destroy humanity — the intellect.

The mind has its place. But God has implanted

89

love in the heart of every human being — even His Son, Christ — so that light shall rise and shine through the mind, giving souls power to comprehend the glories of the universe, bringing salvation to humanity.

Try never to think in terms of 'I' when you have entered the Brotherhood.

The Brotherhood of All Life — a Meditation

May the brotherhood of all life sing in your souls. As we rise to the mountain top to gaze upon the golden sun upon the horizon, we know eternal peace and at-one-ment. We are with our brethren of the great golden lodge above. We know that our feet are set upon a path which will lead unfailingly to the eternal happiness we seek.

We descend to the temple garden and listen to the singing of birds, the language of our animal brethren, the music of the flowers which comes to our senses in perfume and colour. The waving grasses invite us to rest. And we rest....

This is the life of the spirit. God has provided these things for humanity's happiness. Let us live in the spirit, when we can, and bring through into the physical life the inspiration of the true life which is ours. We speak to you from the Brotherhood discarnate. Be of good heart, dear brethren: you are doing great work. Let peace abide, now and always.

CHAPTER 5

With Stars in their Hearts

White Eagle begins by exploring further what we are doing by our work with the light, and how specific words and symbols can be used to hold power for good. He now talks at length about the symbol of the six-pointed Star as a focus, beginning with a description of what he means by light, the substance of which the Star is composed. It is perhaps worth remembering the power White Eagle himself could draw on when he offered the words that follow, in the very speaking of them.

'AND THE MYSTIC words went forth: "Let there be light!".' Think on this. There is a sound-vibration which comes forth from the heart of God and which radiates light, and when you have realized your union with the light within your innermost being you will understand the power of that verse, and when re-peating it you will send forth a sound-vibration into the denser ether that interpenetrates your physical plane. The sending forth from your broadcasting house of a wave of light and love is more potent than any earthly action.

Thus the very first word of creation was 'light'. *Let there be light!* . . . If any of you are sufficiently sensitive you will have felt the vibration which was created as we spoke that word. And we would teach you too that the simple word which is so much used, with so little understanding, the word 'God', has a tremendous power, and the more you send forth the vibration of God, or good, from your thoughts and from your heart, the more you are bringing into active manifestation the power of God. You are bringing it through your own consciousness and projecting it onto the earth plane. Do you begin to see the great power which lies dormant within you? It is the gift of the Creator to you, God's child.

We want you who have offered yourselves in service to humanity continually to send forth, from the powerhouse within the sound-vibration – and not from your lips, but from your innermost being – the vibration of *light*, of *love*. It is of no avail that you read only, or understand intellectually the inner teaching of the Master. The mind of the body will raise queries, will say, 'But what is the use of attempting to interfere with another human's karma? Surely all suffering is self-imposed karma?'

Humanity will need your love. Be constructive in your thought; carry your brethren who are in ignorance of the light, carry them high on your shoulders. You must never turn a deaf ear or a blind eye to suffering and ignorance. The ray of love from your heart may be the light which will lighten that weary wayfarer; it will bind the wounds of the sufferer lying by the wayside, wounded and bleeding from the attack of his enemy. We do not waste words. What the future holds is in God's hands. Look to Him: the all-wise, all-loving Father.

*

Think in terms of light; everything is light. When you think of matter as dark you are keeping it dark, you are increasing its darkness. Think of matter as pulsating light, for this is its true substance when it is held in the mind of Christ, the king of earth's humanity.

Oh, there is much to tell you about the substance and quality of light, and those planes beyond your earth which are created with the substance of light. Without light life would become extinct. Light is life. The light flickers and struggles to stay alight and is only kept alight by the aspirations, the prayers and the good thoughts of the children of God.

Let your light shine, beloved brethren, and you will not want, you will know peace; and when the time comes for you to pass through the portals called death you will walk through with peace in your heart; with joy flooding your souls you will go forward into a world of infinite light and perfection.

You may be part of a small circle only, but around you are countless radiant men and women and angels, and above, shining from the realms of truth, a blazing Star, formed of all the virtues of humanity; all the rays of colour, the tones or notes of music, all the influences of the sacred planets. Each one of you contributes to this blazing Star, some in small and some in great degree. May you, beloved brethren, never forget your service to the Star of Christ, the perfect Son of the Divine Father–Mother God. Whatever humanity receives in blessing, it receives only because it has given its contribution to that Star. Learn to respond to the unseen illumination. Peace be with you all.

*

The Meaning of the Star

SHINING above you is the blazing Star. What is this Star? It is the whole of life. Its rays penetrate through and through humanity, and through the earth plane. In the heart of this blazing Star, this Sun, is the Perfect One, the Son of the Creator, God. Christ is the Son born of the Father–Mother God and sent to earth in human form; sent to earth in the light of love and goodness to raise men and women up from the earth, from darkness into the glory of the spiritual life; into the glory of the heavenly light.

There are countless, countless souls in the Star Circle in the spirit sphere. Their glory is indescribable:

they are beautiful souls. These are they who have come through great tribulation, and have earned the full consciousness of the Christ power. And they live in the ascended state of life. They have reached the goal. They are free, no longer fettered and bound by earth, but they move freely. And they come to earth, and they can leave the earth at will. And they come to their dear brethren to help them upward to that life of freedom and joy and utter bliss.

Such knowledge as this is slowly coming to you. You have a grave responsibility. You are a channel through which the White Brothers are working. It is not easy for you, because you are caught between heaven and earth, dear brethren. But our message to you is to keep your vision upon the glory of the Star. Keep above the material conditions which threaten to bury you. Give your hearts to God and to the Son, Christ your Lord. And then let the magic of the Mighty Sun work. Let it work in your life. It will heal you. It will heal through you. It will restore harmony. It will satisfy all your needs. Have faith! Have faith!

From the faith of the Divine Mother was born the Son.

*

It is the Star of Christ that shines in the heavens at the time of the birth of Christ; and the six-pointed Star is always used for the salvation of humanity.

In your projection of the six-pointed Star to people and countries and across oceans, you can be certain that the light of God is being projected. The Star is a powerful symbol, and if held with love and concentration and devotion to the white light, it will never fail to provide that light, it will never fail to be a focal point to attract the angelic hosts from the Christ spheres who work ceaselessly for the Christ power to manifest on earth. Where the Star shines by the will and through the love of earthly men and women, the effect over chaos and disorder, over war and all the evils that derive from it, is truly amazing.

The six-pointed Star is the most beautiful and perfect symbol of the perfectly balanced human being, the one who has his or her head in the heavens, whose faculties are quickened, awakened to the reception of God life, and whose feet are firmly planted upon the road of earth which he or she traverses – with one object in view, which is to find and give absolute happiness.

We will hear many explanations of the six-pointed Star symbol, but the phrase we heard on p. 95, 'it is the whole of life' will always resonate through them. Elsewhere, White Eagle calls it 'God's plan for humanity ... the symbol of creation'.* He now offers help in attunement to the Star,

*See the collection, PRAYER, MINDFULNESS AND INNER CHANGE (Liss, Hants., 2003, p. 52)

for (as he will tell us) it is more than an object of concentration; rather, a living force.

Brethren, in the great silence of God you will find power, love and wisdom. In the midst of the turmoil of today you should strive to reach this sanctuary of silence. It is beyond the reach of the mind – it lies within the depths of the heart of love....

Those who would be of use to the Master must strive to attain a measure of peace within. We have spoken of the love within your breast, and the necessity for love to guide and inspire all your work. But we impress also upon you the power of peace. Peace is a dynamic force, a creative power, and without peace in your hearts you lose power. Love, too, is dynamic, but it loses its force if there is no peace. Conduct yourselves, your life, your work, with the eternal peace in your heart. If you would help your fellow men and women, maintain peace within.

We understand how difficult it is for you, moving in the world, to retain inner tranquillity. You speak of peace, you pray for peace, you seek peace on earth. The way to realize this ideal is to live in tranquillity yourself. Tranquillity is not easy to attain, particularly in the busy city and harassed by the constant disturbance and irritation of the massed thought of humanity. We have learnt from experience that the way to attain the tranquil spirit is to surrender life and all its emotions to God. Then the balm of tranquillity flows into the soul, brother or sister is at peace.

*

If you wish to direct the Star of healing to the nations it is a little difficult, we notice, for some of you to focus the light in the right way. You just think of words. Do not think in this way. We suggest that it will help you if you feel the light in your heart and let it go forth as if it is expanding from your heart, and direct it upon the centres of government of the countries to which you are directing the light....

So it is not wise to indulge in nebulous thought or feeling when you are projecting the light. We give you the focal point from which to work. When you go onto the inner planes you close the door and enter the inner sanctuary, close the door on material things, outer-world things. You go into the sanctuary of the spirit and seek contact with the Star.

The Star is the source of light to all human souls. In the ancient brotherhoods it was recognized as the Pole Star, the Star by which the mariner steers the ship. It is the symbol of the Christ life, which is the Star of human life. You are the captains of your ship, of your soul, and you guide your soul over the rough seas of life by the light of the Pole Star, which in turn is the six-pointed Star, the symbol of the Christ, the perfectly balanced man–woman, the human being who is poised between heaven and earth. The human side reaches up in the one triangle and in the other the Christ side descends and perfectly interpenetrates the human.

When you go onto the inner planes, my dear ones, you will find there a great light, impossible to describe in human words. Get in your mind's eye the form of the Christ, the perfect man and woman, the perfect dual soul. See this as the very heart of a blazing star, a blazing sun, for it draws close to you, so close that it becomes a blazing sun, and in the whiteness and the golden rays of that sun you perceive the human form, the perfect son–daughter of the living God. Get this focused in your heart; dwell on this picture and say to yourself, 'Christ within me is the resurrection and the life'. Then feel that life rising in you, illuminating your head and your whole being.... You will feel the power of this light coursing through your being and you will feel a great love towards all life. Then in your personal disappointments in life you will feel an acceptance and a love. You will know that God is good and wise and all-loving. You will feel God's power enfolding you and raising you from the limitations that you chafe at, right up into the freedom and opportunities that you long for.

One key thing about the Star is that we can see it externally if we wish, even with our physical eyes: a star in the heavens, brighter maybe than any other object in the night sky. Or we can see it shining above us in thought: inspiring, guiding, protecting us. We can see it just in front of us, and feel its warmth (a lovely way to send healing is to hold the form of the Star before us, and imagine its light radiating out). Best of all, though, as the previous passage reminds us, is not to separate it in any way from our deepest being; in reality, because we have God within, because we are God, then we are also the Star. We have the two triangles within us.

The next passage refers to a three-dimensional glass crystal star of great beauty, which the White Eagle Brotherhood was given at the beginning of its work. It is a symbol of something much vaster and brighter. As this section ends, White Eagle also comments on the rose, which is also traditionally placed on the altar during a service in his Lodge.

Beloved brethren, will you visualize the blazing crystal Star which hangs before the altar, *within your own being*? Visualize it and hold fast to the vision; see it radiating countless rays of light....

Now imagine the effect of such a light in the darkness upon your earth. Imagine the power of an earthly light; think of the warmth and the life-force which such a light would give out. Yet a physical or material lamp would only be a shell, something quite tawdry in comparison to the pulsating, living Star. We want you to think of this, so that you may catch some idea of the immense amount of work that the Star, when powerfully and steadily projected into the ether which interpenetrates the physical, can do.

The power of thought is infinite. It has been proved again and again by psychologists. Cannot you see how much stronger can be the thought if it is animated by spiritual light? We want to give this message, not only to you, my brethren, but through you to all the world, to all who will listen and will benefit by this knowledge. We know that the world is hard and materialistic, that people base all their calculations and place all their faith in material things. But there are many who have reached the point in their evolution where they can be awakened to spiritual truths.

Consider the construction of the Star, which is perfectly balanced. The six-pointed Star cannot be reversed. Whichever way you turn it and whichever way you use it, it remains six-pointed, perfectly balanced, like the perfect symbol of a balanced life. The six-pointed Star is an ancient symbol and one of the most powerful which is used in white magic. It is only used in white magic – and in this it differs from the pentagram, which can be reversed.

We would impress upon you once again the need for perfect balance and equilibrium, one of the five great cosmic laws. The six-pointed Star is a perfect symbol of that balance, balance between matter and spirit. The trouble in the present world is that there is no balance – it is all matter, which is used without the introduction of an equal quantity of spiritual light and power. It would not do for the world to be all spirit, either: for people to be all spirit and there be no physical or material form to bring about the balance. The perfect life of God is this perfect interpenetration, where matter is the vehicle through which the spirit manifests.

*

You may wonder why we so often draw your attention to the symbol of the rose. Every symbol creates a vibration on the ether and the rose sends out waves of love. The very thought of a sweetly-scented rose brings a feeling of love, and if you smell that rose with your physical senses you feel within you a beautiful sense of harmony and peace and love. When brethren feel this love in their hearts and then commence their work of thought projection, the form of the Star which they are projecting becomes a living and most powerful object. It becomes alive with spirit. Remember that thought creates form, but the love in your heart gives life to that form and sends it forth, and it reaches its mark.

Commitment to the work of the Star, to the Brotherhood of the Star, is a tremendous privilege but it also brings commitment. Who would ever want to feel that the salvation of all humanity, which the Brotherhood teaches by example and promotes by projecting the Star, did not happen because we lost interest in our work? In a particularly beautiful teaching, White Eagle speaks of the importance of remaining positive and committed, but also reminds us that in brotherhood everyone is on an equal footing. To preserve that sense requires great discipline and discrimination, a constant setting-aside of the pride held by the ego and devoting oneself to the many.

Do not underestimate the importance of this brotherhood work: do not underestimate it, we beg you. God must be your vision. God must be your horizon, and the Master your companion leading you upwards towards the eternal light and glory and crown of life. Resolutely refuse to think negatively, however difficult your life may be at times. We know we are giving you true, sound advice. Always look to the light and be positive about the good coming, because that is surely the eventual goal of every life. As you allow negative thoughts to pull you down you suffer unnecessarily. When you allow thoughts of the God-power to flow into you, you are lifted nearer your goal. One is death and the other is life. You want to live and you need your physical body for a long life of service on the earth plane.

You all have a mission and you cannot judge the greatness or otherwise of that mission. You do not know how far the light strikes as it flows through you. It is well that you do not know. All brothers of the Star are united in the work of projecting the Light. No one is more important than another; you are as one. You should aim at this unity and aim at thinking of yourselves as the blazing Star in the Lodge. You are one, *you are one*, dear brethren.

We say this with all love. The power of the Brotherhood, the power of the Star, is magical. The magic of the Star is love, and only when a brother or sister is full of love for God and humankind will the magic work. The magic is not self-will, it is love.

*

Once, a great brother whose teachings are known all over the world today, said, 'I am simply holding up the Light for others to see by'. We would like you to remember that you and we are gathered about the radiant Star of brotherhood – and are holding it aloft with courage and love in our hearts; and the love from our hearts is illuminating the Star, and causing its rays to shine all over the earth. The rays of this Star of brotherhood will shine for many centuries. We have no complicated ways, no intricate mental paths, but we all have banded together to hold aloft the radiant Star of our brotherhood, and have nothing else in our hearts but brotherhood and love, for we know that love is the thing which will cast fear out of men and women.

It is not enough, though, that we think of the Star of brotherhood, and do all we can to hold the Star aloft. We must endeavour to remember the laws of brotherhood in our human contacts one with the other. It is so easy for us to talk from spirit, we know; so easy for you just to listen. But shall we all try, once more, to guard our lips, and before speaking, say: 'Is it kind? Is it going to be helpful to my brother, or is it going to hurt him? Is it going to help my brother on the path of service and brotherhood, or is it going to cast him down, and make his journey a little more difficult? Will what I am going to say be a burden to my sister's back, one more little straw for her to carry, or will it put light into her eyes and wings to her feet, and cause her to walk her path with joy?'

*

The Star of the Self

The Star is more than a symbol, as we have seen: rather, a living entity that is universal: at once all and part of life. It is also something to internalize, inasmuch as the more we become the Star the more it radiates visibly from us. Here White Eagle begins by giving a whole new dimension to brotherhood while returning in his symbolism to the guiding star of the mariner. In the passage, we find that 'Star' and 'brotherhood' are inextricable.

WE HAVE spoken many times of the vast brotherhood of life, the brotherhood of all races past – and the brotherhood of yourself. We spoke of the numbers of personalities which made up your own soul,

and told you why you were linked with thes
personalities which were your own. This, you
agree, is a tremendous realization – that we o
selves are a community, and that there are communities linked with communities which form spheres,
and that there are planes upon planes of consciousness which form worlds.

The whole of life is a brotherhood, but the
world does not recognize this cosmic truth. Your
brotherhood is one of many similar groups which
exist, which have existed through all ages. The Polar Star guides the mariner on the ocean and, when
spiritually interpreted, it is the Star in the centre of
your heaven, the Star everyone has, no matter who
or what they are. It has been called by other names,
and one of these names is said to be conscience. But
it is even deeper than conscience – it urges you to be
as the Grand Master of your Lodge.

The Grand Master of your life, as you all know,
is the Beloved: the perfect one, Christ, the on-
ly-begotten Son of the Father–Mother God. We are
speaking of the light which is born of the Father–
Mother God and which takes its place within the
soul of every created human being. Because of this,
every human being is related to the Father–Mother
God as a son. This creates the perfect trinity: Father,
Mother, Son. You all know this, but it is well to repeat well-known truths.

This trinity can be likened to the golden triangle which points downwards into matter to stimulate and to create in matter a similar triangle; when this lower triangle becomes impregnated with the light and radiance of the higher triangle, we behold the Star.

This happens too when the lower elements in you rise and become illumined by the true light of the golden triangle, pointing down. Then it is that the Polar Star, the Star which is in the heavens, takes possession and guides you on a course which is safe and sure and true.

*

Now within you is the potentiality to become such a master soul, and you are beginning on earth at this very moment. This is not a fairy tale; it is scientifically true. You send out light and on the etheric plane you build a Star, and the rays from that Star travel. At the same time you, individually, are building within your soul the form of the six-pointed Star, the double triangle in perfect balance. It is so simple: as the Christ Light within you becomes strong through love and service, so the form of the body is enveloped in the form of the Star, and that Star is sending forth rays. So, my brother, my sister, as you move about the world, which is your universe, you are radiating the Christ Light. You do not need to open your lips, you do not need to speak at all. You are, by your radiation, touching your brother and

sister. Your aura is radiating from you. ˈ
of the light is the work of a brother oˌ
er with practical service to the physical anɑ ˌˌ
needs, which must be given every moment of lıˌ
and given perfectly as the Star is built in you.

Only the light can dispel darkness, and there is
a good deal of darkness abroad. It can only be dis-
pelled by the light of the spirit, the light which burns
in your hearts. And the light must rise into the mental planes so that you are able to comprehend the
work of projecting and radiating light. Your work
is to stimulate – in those dark hearts embodied in
flesh – the wisdom of working co-operatively and
constructively and selflessly: not working for one
section of the community alone, but working for the
spiritual emancipation of all humanity.

Do not become lax or weary. Band together in
spirit and work from the higher Lodge, the counterpart of the earthly one. Seek its door; go through the
door of the higher lodge of the Star and work there
in your sleep and beneath your everyday consciousness, and remember that on this inner plane there
is no limitation of time or space. Make contact, just
for a flash, with the thought of the brethren assembled round the altar with the light upon it: just think
of this many times during the day and especially last
thing at night, and direct your soul to go to the temple of the Star, and you will go there. You will in

time stimulate the brain and the memory and you will know in your physical waking consciousness that you have been working with the Brotherhood of the Star on the inner planes.

Work with the Star demands absolute respect for others, for ultimately all religions are part of the same work.
We lay stress on this, my brethren: always respect another's religion. Always be courteous about another's religion and never force your opinions or religious beliefs upon another, for there are many different paths to the sacred altar. You have chosen your path; the brother and the sister by your side have chosen their path – *respect it.*

This is a feature in all the elder brethren. All the great teachers you could name, who are met in the Great White Lodge, are strictly courteous and respectful one to another, for all realize their one common source, all realize that every teacher comes to the world at a certain time for a certain purpose, and when humanity is at a certain stage of spiritual development, where it can absorb only so much and no more. All religions then should be respected, for there is only one true and perfect religion, and all humankind have this one religion in their hearts. It is the religion of the Star ... *the Star! the Light!* The Light of the Son, the Son of God.

*

If you would be truly a brother or sister of the Star, you are love, you are radiating love, you are a loving, compassionate, considerate, kind soul. All the virtues of the Star are manifested in you.

How do you approach the Star? Not through your minds: you bring the power of the divine will and love to send forth the Light. You are brother or sister in deed, in thought, in speech. We are not preaching. We are merely stating a truth. When a large company of incarnate souls are sending forth, through their heart and life, the light of the Star, the very stones of the earth will cry out. There will be a complete revolution of life from the material to the spiritual. It will be the spiritualization of matter, and that necessarily means a raising of the vibrations of matter until they become purer and finer, until they get beyond death and destruction. You know these things in your heart. We remind you of them from time to time to encourage you and to help you to go forward with your work and to look upward to the apex of the diamond, to the heart of the Star....

Finally, a note on group work, and a reminder that through our refusal to subscribe to the concept of human separateness, we open ourselves to the same qualities that enable us to work with the Star — openness of heart, sympathy, recognition of the individual worth of another, of every one of the infinitely diverse beings that populate earth. The group White Eagle speaks of is of course the one he works with in the White Eagle Lodge, but his words are once again applicable to groups of light workers everywhere.

There is great radiation of light from such a group as this. We emphasize this fact because the group work is all-important: through group work so much more is accomplished than in isolation. You will not only look out towards the light, but you will realize the quickening and the unfoldment of the light within your own heart and you will overcome separation. We have said many times that where there is love there is no separation. My brethren, *this is the destiny of the human race: in time, to overcome separation.*

There is great stress laid upon individualization. This is a step on the evolutionary path, but it is only a step, for after self-realization must come unification, the overcoming of separateness, and the brotherhood of the White Light. Work towards this end: the overcoming of separation, the unification of life, the building of universal brotherhood.

*

Beloved brethren, behold above you a blazing Star! It shines from the heavens upon this earth planet and there are only small groups who are so receptive to its rays they can transmit them. The Brotherhood of the Star was formed in the invisible world long before you were on the earth. You have no conception yet of the vastness of this Brotherhood. You are, as

yet, entirely unaware of the numbers of Star brethren, not only out of the body and around this earth
planet, but many, many who are working in the finer
ethers around other planets in your solar system....

We would have our dear brethren here hold
their vision on the Star and see in that symbol the
perfect harmony, the perfect balance and interpenetration of the pair of opposites. This is a truth which
all souls must in due time comprehend.

Now this work is penetrating slowly but surely.
On the inner planes it is helping to bring about such
balance, and to establish the goodwill among the nations which must and will come. It will slowly come
until there is one commonwealth of nations, with all
humankind recognizing the needs of their brothers
and sisters on Earth (and we hear one of the elder
brethren whispering: 'and the recognition of all the
gifts of God, Brother Air, Brother Water and the Lord
of the Sun'). Try to comprehend the love of the Great
One who gave these gifts, and worship Him–Her.
When human beings can do this, and rise above the
level of self, then they will surely know the meaning
of peace, and happiness and fulfilment; but while the
self dominates, there can only be frustration.

Brethren, hold fast together in one spirit, giving
of yourselves all the gifts that God has given you for
the blessing and the healing of your brethren.

In the Temple of the Star

Beloved brethren, we would, all together, rise and enter the temple of the blazing golden Star. May we all understand the power of this heavenly place, this heart of life, this centre within the golden Star. In silence, brethren, let us all assemble within this radiance, this golden radiance, and commune with the Son of God, the Solar Logos … the life, the love, the wisdom and the power of life which is yours now and at all times. We would have you understand, we would have you be aware of the power and the glory of the life in the Star; the symbol of the new age of humanity on the earth planet. You, who have given yourselves to the service of the Star, must realize the power and the life of the Star. It is spirit, it is truth, it is all, it is all in all.

May every brother and sister who comes to work together use this divine power to serve life on the earth plane, and life on the astral plane surrounding the earth. At this moment remember those who have passed from you into the world of light … and be now at one with them and with all souls in the Star. All love, all love reigns in the heart and centre of the Star.

Hear from the temples of the past the chant of the sun! *All hail, all hail, Thou art the Sun, the Life!*

CHAPTER 6

Being a Brother

White Eagle begins with a reminder of the work that all who use the White Eagle Lodge as their way of setting out on the path are asked to perform. This is to create a moment of stillness at every one of the cardinal points in the waking hours (that is, at 3.00, 6.00, 9.00 and 12.00), and during this time simply to allow a feeling that the light of spirit, entering us, streams forth to reach anywhere there is need. In some cases this will be to a list of people who have actually asked for healing. The love in the human heart is what enables this light to break through every crust that may surround the personality. The Star adds focus.

The commandment about loving God with heart, soul and mind is from Matthew 22:37 and Luke 10:27.

YOU ARE CALLED to an unusual service in this Brotherhood. Many would not understand working on the mental plane, on the inner spiritual plane, but the work of the Star Brotherhood is just this. You work continually on the inner planes. You work from the light of Christ in your heart.

The light of Christ is symbolized by the Star of the perfectly balanced soul. The Brotherhood is working for man or woman made perfect through the manifestation of the Christ in the heart, causing the thoughts and the actions to be as near to the Christlike as possible. It means that the life is lived in service to your fellow creatures. At the magical hours during the day – 3.00, 6.00, 9.00 and 12.00 – by an effort of love and the divine will, you project the light of the Star into the world. This work has not been done on the earth planet in such a way for a very, very, long time.

It is the forerunner of a new work for humanity. It is the beginning, but it is the same work on the soul plane of humanity which will eventually raise the whole system of human life. There will be complete evolution, spiritual evolution of life on your earth, and it will come from the seed which is now being sown in the minds and consciousness of humanity. You will see the radiation of this light and power throughout humankind.

We repeat, from the Masters in the higher worlds, that you are the pioneers of a new religion. We will admit no doubts! It is by the will of God that the work of brotherhood has been instituted on the earth, and by the will of God it will increase all over the world.

*

You all know that in treading the spiritual path, truly you cannot advance without your influence and light affecting the lives of all humanity. With every step forward that you as an individual take, you are as-

116

sisting all humanity to rise towards the light. Therefore the discarnate brethren who come to you from the spiritual realms so gladly give to you their loving service in your earthly pilgrimage. It is not you alone they help – they have learnt that in helping you, they help all people.

We would have you do likewise in your life: go about the earth *being* love, being brotherly, not only to those who are congenial to you but to all. It is too easy to love those who love us; the Master teaches us to love our enemies. As we have said, *all human beings are your teachers*. If you learn from your brethren, you are very glad to say, 'Thank you, sister. Thank you, brother'. This seems to be a wise attitude of mind. God is omnipotent and all-wise, and holds humanity in His–Her heart and mind. It is our work continually to express love – not to condemn, not to resent, not to fear, but to live peacefully, knowing that all moves forward to the desired culmination.

You all have responsibilities of a material and spiritual nature. There is only one law, one commandment – 'Love the Lord your God with all your heart and all your soul and all your mind'. Love God first, love all that is good in the world, love all that is good in life, see good in life; love God, love good with all your heart and soul and mind. And so doing, you must love your neighbour as yourself.

*

This is not a modern brotherhood; it is exceedingly ancient and, my dear brothers and sisters, it is your privilege and your sacred obligation to preserve the sanctity of the brotherhood work. Be a channel for this divine power and distribute it with tender love. Open your heart to the Christ love. Send out the Star from the heart centre to all those you meet whom you can see are in pain and trouble. Just in a brief flash of time lift them up in the heart of the Star.

We would remind you, though, that you cannot effectively do your work unless you are in attunement with the brotherhood and with all life. There must be no disquieting note in brotherhood. You must always regard your brethren as your brethren. Never see anything else but good in them. See the good, the true and the beautiful. In this way, my children, by this practice of seeing good as well as doing good, you are helping in the upliftment and the healing of all peoples.

After a few more words about symbols, four of the basic rules of the earthly Brotherhood are now set out. Although called 'rules', they are idealistic and there may be a timescale of some duration before their full realization. Yet the true brother or sister takes such ideals seriously, so the word 'rules' is not inappropriate.

We would speak of the Star Brotherhood, now formed on earth. A group of men and women have

118

been drawn together, not by any mental allegiance, not by any intellectual urge, but by their common humanity, by the spirit within them. The spirit, or God, or the divine man–woman, is thus manifesting in human souls, and this spirit is symbolized by the six-pointed Star. The complete symbol of this Brotherhood is a Star at the centre of a cross. The cross is the oldest symbol known, and represents the human being as he or she stands, with feet together and head erect: feet upon the earth, head in the heavens, and arms stretched forth in service and in sacrifice. Yet when humanity begins to recognize the spirit of divinity within all people, their service to each of their brethren becomes no longer sacrifice but joy. And so the cross is a symbol of sacrifice, service and joy.

Surrounding, enfolding the cross, is the circle, the universal circle of light and love, the ancient astrological symbol of the sun. The sun, or the spiritual counterpart of the sun, shines in the heart of the true brother–sister, so that others walking along life's pathway may be lighted by the sunlight in that one's heart.

The spirit of love, which has awakened in the heart, draws the individual into service. Therefore, he or she endeavours to order life under the guidance and mastership of that divinity within. For the individual has learnt by then that in common with all humanity he or she is a divine son or daughter of the Almighty, the dual spirit, male and female, Father–Mother God. As a child of God, and by illumining the mind with divine intelligence, the individual orders life so as to be continually receptive to the divine light guiding his or her actions. The individual meditates upon his or her true status in life, upon the wonders and glories of creation and of the universe in which he or she lives. Having realized that she is part of a universe of spiritual beauty and power and wisdom, this sister seeks to learn more of that greater wisdom beyond the mortal life, beyond the understanding of the earth mind; that brother learns that there is a mind in his heart which some call the intuition. The approaching age will demonstrate to humanity that this sixth sense of the human race is stirring, is awakening.

It is the work of those in the White Brotherhood to cleanse and purify the body. Brethren recognize that coarse living and coarse feeding also coarsen the very structure of the aura and body. How can the divine Spirit or the Master function through a body clogged with unsuitable food, or deadened by narcotics and drugs? Or when it is unable to breathe, not only the fresh air, but all the vibrations of the higher ethers about us?

So one of the first rules for the aspirant is to eat pure food – and not only this, but to eat with thankfulness to the Creator. We are always telling brethren not to become ascetics – to be natural, to eat in plenty of the beautiful fruits of the earth, and green vegetables and whole grains, and to eat all the natural foods in which the body delights, and will enjoy. These foods will purify and cleanse the physical body and the aura, and raise humanity's consciousness to behold the beauties of the universe.

The Star brother or sister lives not for him- or herself, but strives meekly and humbly to think of others. Self-will, the unbridled ego which would assert itself and overrule others, has to be subdued. Until the unruly part is subdued, none of you may enter into the kingdom of heaven. This is indeed a practical religion which the White Lodge above endeavours to introduce.

The third rule of the White Brotherhood is that the brother or sister lives to comfort those who mourn, and to give sympathy and understanding to those in sorrow, even if it be seen that the suffering has been brought by foolishness and ignorance. It is not the work of the brother or sister to criticize another but to help the one suffering to pick up their burden. He or she may say, 'My brother, my sister, there is a reason for your suffering – all suffering is the result of the law of cause and effect. But we will not dwell upon this, but rather give you all the help we can'.

The brother or sister would serve humankind in a practical way, give help of a practical and, if necessary, a financial nature, at all times. He or she would understand sorrow, the great darkness and loneliness of bereavement. By attunement to the spheres of truth and light, communion can be held with the Beloved.

We tell you that the souls of illumined men and women are drawing closer, helping humanity to clear away the mists of materialism and folly. They help human beings to live harmoniously with one another, and to establish peace on earth and a true brotherhood. The brother–sister of the Star will not tolerate the sufferings of his or her lowly brethren; will not be content to see fellow men and women materially exploited and outraged; will work to better the conditions of all beings throughout the world. Sharing as he or she does in a true brotherhood of the spirit, recognizing the needs of all humanity, each one so orders his or her life as to be of help, and does not hinder the progress of any brother or sister on the path.

The four rules now set out, White Eagle explains ways in which they may operate: in effect, the self-discipline that brotherhood asks of us — but also the basic principle of brotherhood itself, which is love for others.

In the first passage, some instructions are set out in a way that also touches on the ancient origins of brotherhood today.

There is a natural earthly reaction to the faults and

failings of those around you, but we bring you a message from the Brotherhood, the eternal brotherhood. It is not new to you. It has been given on a former occasion from our brothers in Tibet. These are the words: 'Talk with your brother of the ideals and aims of the Brotherhood; be one with your brother in time of joy and sorrow, entering into these things with your brother; but be deaf and dumb and blind to all things outside the triangle of true Brotherhood'.*

This means that you have one great thing in common, the brotherhood ideal, the service you can render in your own simple and humble way to the evolution of humanity and the bringing into all hearts the happiness and the joy of true brotherhood. Be blind, deaf and dumb to anything outside this. We cannot judge anyone. We do not know their karma, and when we have reached the stage where we can see beyond the veil, when we can see the karma of our brothers, we shall only feel intense love for them. We cannot judge the action of others. We see only the outworking of the law of karma by which they are compelled to live.

This message we have given first of all by the wish of our brethren in the East, and secondly to

*This quotation is set out here in White Eagle's actual words at the time, although a slightly different phrasing may be familiar to members of the White Eagle Lodge.

questions in the hearts of the brothers and in the physical body. Your rule resolves itself in the one word – love. Love and be tolerant and wide in your sympathy. Judge not, for no one can judge another.

Love, love, love. So easy to say; you may think it is a platitude, but it is the foundation of life. If you were ready to be taken into the ashram of the Master you would have lessons given you in this very step and you would have very difficult tasks to perform. You are trying to do this in the world. The western world is not an easy place to find God, but the soul who can find God in the midst of the materialism of the western world is developing rapidly that wisdom and love combined.

You have a great opportunity to develop this gentle Christ spirit in the very midst of the hard materialism of your world in the West. In this brittle mental age – which is going to be a great tester as well as a great teacher and revealer of the inner mysteries of nature – all the secrets of nature, the earth, the sky, the etheric worlds, the physical body and the secrets of the finer bodies of men and women are going to be unfolded. If you put material things and material organization first, you will fail, though: you will crash. You will be trying to put on a roof before your foundations are well and truly laid.

Developing love in the heart, love for one's brei
is the greatest rule of brotherhood — holds
It also helps in the development of a clear visiv...,
where there is love, understanding is never very far behind.
The second aspect of our work from spirit is to teach
humanity about its own inner powers. The principal
gift is clairvoyance, clear vision, which means far
more than seeing spirits. It means seeing *Spirit*, the
spirit of God, of Christ, in another soul. It means
penetrating the mists of materiality and earthliness
and going through from your world into the heavenly states of life, penetrating with your vision beyond
the earth plane to other planets in the solar system.
Humanity is quite unaware as yet of the immensity
of the unfoldment which will take place within every human being.

We want you to learn to draw aside the veil between physical matter and the astral plane and the
mental plane and the celestial plane so that in your
own way, by your own freewill, you can rise and
live on these other invisible planes of life. The salvation of this earth depends on the power of love
to transform the life of pain and suffering to a life
of harmony and brotherhood, beauty and wisdom.
When the balance between the heart and the head in
humankind is achieved, the way will be opened for
the visitation not only of angels, but of friends from
outer space. If only we could persuade you that by

living the life of the spirit, by devoting your prayers and service to the spirit, you can raise the whole world from darkness to light!

Taken from a public talk, some of the next passage has been quoted many times in the White Eagle Lodge, as the phrase 'to bring to earth a standard of life which is in harmony with the infinite love' is the basis of many of the statements the Lodge has made about its mission on earth. The phrase nonetheless has to be carefully considered in context in order to understand the range of meaning it holds.

We want you to understand (again we emphasize this) that you who listen are all being guided; no soul is ever forced to join the White Eagle Lodge or to become a member of the brotherhood at its heart. Instead, opportunities are placed before you which, if you accept them, will help you to progress. You will progress by what is called 'initiation' – or by a series of initiations. Remember, however, that what you call initiations are really experimental: we do not always know how a soul will react to its initiation, or if it will avail itself of its new opportunity. It may react nobly and gain great good; but if not, it may have to await a further opportunity. Initiation therefore means an opportunity for expansion of consciousness and spiritual growth.

When we speak of 'the Great White Lodge' in we mean a centre, temple or lodge within a city of light, where assemble souls who have gained considerable spiritual knowledge. Beyond these are the hierarchies whose work it is to oversee or watch over the needs of humanity – the spiritual needs, yes, and also the physical and material needs. Do not imagine that the hierarchies of heaven are unaware of the ordinary everyday requirements of human beings. If you understood the workings of the laws of karma, and if you realized that the Lords of Karma watch over the application of these laws even down to the simplest details on the physical plane, you would be overwhelmed with wonder and with joy.

Of course, freewill choice is never infringed; humankind can react as it likes. Only when people have earned their new opportunities is it the work of the Lords of Karma to direct them into the paths of opportunity. Thus, what you may call miracles are really the result of the operation of this spiritual karmic law. Such progress always means sacrifice; and that is why human beings always have within themselves power to forge ahead if they are willing to make the sacrifice required.

The particular master responsible for bringing this Lodge into being is one whom you know quite well, but often by different names, for he has many aspects. He is working for the great brotherhood of the new age. In the past he has established through the centuries schools of knowledge, schools of the inner mysteries, and brought about all kinds of reforms. His particular work today is to establish a brotherhood founded upon the family spirit, founded upon love. He still retains a body, and so can manifest in different parts of the world when it is necessary, but only to help people accomplish a certain piece of work which is vitally important. We want you to realize that our Lodge has behind it a fine purpose. That purpose extends far into the future: it is to bring to earth *a standard of life which is in harmony with the infinite love.* The Lodge is not therefore a place for complex expositions of intellectual truth. It is instead ever working to stimulate the simple human love in every heart.

As a rule, whenever people congregate, you get dissension, because the love between them is not strong enough. It is then that the mind gets to work and overcomes the tender growth of love. The purpose of the work here is brotherhood — and through brotherhood, through sympathy, patience and tolerance one with another, you are learning to establish a universal brotherhood.

Can you believe that all souls at heart long for harmony, and so long for God? That is because all souls belong to God. Each one of you here is a child of God. Within your heart is the Christ child. You are yourself a potential Christ child. The Christ child is symbolized by the rose, because of its fragrance and

128

beauty. The old type of rose had to be pr[...]
thorns, which caused anyone to handle the [...]
great care. The rose, then, is the symbol of t[...]
Christ love in the human heart, and this must [...]
handled with great care. It can be a little prickly, as
you are all finding out! You must learn to be tender
with the heart of another, so that neither you nor
the other person will be hurt. The rose is perfect
in form and opens its petals to the sun. The human
heart is perfectly formed in God's own image, and
will always, *always*, respond to the sunlight of truth,
to the sunlight of God.

In the forming of this Lodge the master has laid
down the rule of love, and in giving freedom to all,
has thereby called upon each to respond in the finest, the truest manner. Our master's one theme,
the key of all his work, has been to bring light, to
stimulate the light which already lies in the hearts
of those drawn into the orbit of his work. We can
witness through the centuries the noble work of this
great master, which has always been to introduce to
humanity the truth of God, the light within. For this
alone can be humanity's salvation, and this development in each one of you will bring into your lives
harmony, health, opportunity, great beauty, and in-
expressible happiness and joy.

Expanded Awareness

*

The Discipline of the Brotherly Life

Put aside all thoughts other than love. Cultivate a sense of humour! Laugh! And above all, awaken! Awaken, my brethren, to the great reality of life — and this is God, happiness. Live intensely, joyously; you are not separated; only as you yourselves separate yourselves by wrong thinking.

*

We who work with you are so happy to see the efforts towards self-discipline in all of you. You are quite safe in looking to the spiritual life for companionship and guidance and help. This interpretation of the two worlds is intended so that humankind is uplifted and able to receive brethren from other spheres. Such brethren possess physical bodies of a much higher rate of vibration than the physical, earthly body. The trend of the whole universe is towards this spiritual evolution. We often say, keep your balance, but that does not mean that you have to remain fastened to the earth. It means that you retain your balance through goodness and love and kindness towards humanity and towards all creation.

*

Now we are going to give you a very simple formula for finding the path of truth. It is this: daily to live thankfully. It is very simple, so simple that few have attained this way of living. As soon as a heart beats with thankfulness, first of all for its creation, secondly for its preservation, and thirdly for all experiences that befall it, no matter what they are, that soul causes a light to shine forth from the very centre of its being, an ancient light. All mystics understand this light; all brethren of the White Brotherhood who have been taught in the mystic schools of the ages have understood the opening of the heart centre.

This centre of the heart is opened gradually and by degrees. In all there are seven degrees before the heart centre is fully open and the power of the white fire and magic can be used to the glory of the Father, Mother and Son. This is a very ancient mystery of which we speak, of which you know nothing as yet; but within that drawing out lies the mystery, the secret of life from the beginning to the end and through cycle after cycle of life. The very act of being thankful, of never seeing anything in life as too difficult, but accepting all life's experiences, and above all, life itself – the very joy of breathing, the joy of speaking, of singing, of hearing, of tasting – even these simple gifts so often unrecognized by us all should invoke an outpouring of thankfulness from within. Instead of this there is much criticism, much disagreement with life, and consequently the heart remains shuttered – although deep within it is

ight, which flickers and only occasionally
th.

is within each one of us the power to cause
that heart centre to expand and cause it to be as a
magnet to receive the forces of the Sun, the glorious
Sun of life – the Christ nature in humanity. Open,
then, this heart of yours in thankfulness for life and
everything that life brings!

We know that the burdens of life weary the flesh
and the mind, but these burdens should be swept
away when the heart is open in thankfulness for
their coming, and for the sweetness and the beauty
which they will unfold through the thankful heart.

Now, peace be with you, true, deep peace, peace
which whispers to you, 'All is well, all is well in my
life. If I am well there is no other thing than peace'.

*

No other man or woman can tell us our duty: it is
for us to find that way for ourselves. This is true
brotherhood. Ponder well, think well, and resolve
to keep on keeping on up the hill. Turn your faces to the light, and the light will stream down, my
brother, my sister: so warm, so glorious. Thus, without realizing it, you will find that you have helped a
whole string of weary travellers upon their way. You
will have shared with them your spiritual food, as
did Jesus with the bread and the fish fed to the five
thousand. Is not Jesus through his faithful followers

132

now on earth continually feeding the masses – feeding, not the five thousand only, but thousands upon thousands – even millions? This spirit of sharing, of helpfulness, of brotherhood, we must keep alive. We must apply this truth to every department of life.

Despite our use of terms like 'discipline' and 'self-discipline', White Eagle is never over-prescriptive in his teaching. Indeed, much of it being about thought rather than action, he stresses qualities of mind that it is good to hold. The story he takes to illustrate this is, once again, from St John's Gospel (chapter 8).

Remember that in life it is desirable always to retain elasticity of mind. It is impossible to confine or bind truth. You must allow a wide margin. It is not wise to assert, 'Lo, here is truth!' or 'Lo, there is truth!' Rather feel that truth is everywhere, and if human life, or your contact with life, seems to fall short of your truth, perhaps your ideal may be false. Lay it aside; see truth working through every experience of life. Never be too rigid; and judge no one. '*Woman, hath no man condemned thee?*' 'No one, Lord!' '*Neither do I condemn thee!*' May we always bear these words in mind.... And when we reach that stage in which we never feel other than love and gentleness towards life, we begin to lose that sense of separation – for behold, in love there is no separation!

*

133

Two words we leave in your minds. The first is patience – one of the most difficult lessons to be learnt. Do you know that in the spheres of the spirit life impatience holds many a soul back? And in the past, in the inner mystery schools, the candidate was always taught the inadvisability of rushing forward too quickly, because by being too eager to enter the light he or she might be blinded. Therefore you must work patiently with chisel and gavel upon the rough ashlar of your being, which you cannot hope to perfect without long and patient work. Learn patience, and you will enter into that peace which gives power.

The second word is love. Perhaps you think we should have put love first? But patience is necessary in order to learn love. In simple human language, may we beg you to *strive for love*? Love is not sentiment or emotion. Love is of the spirit, and by it you recognize the spirit in your brother and sister. Love refrains from judgment – never attributes wrong motives to another. God alone knows the hearts of your brethren. It is so easy to misjudge. Refrain always. If you do not understand, know that the time will come when you *will* understand the reason for certain things happening.

Without love all power is self-consuming. The fires of power will consume the soul; the warmth of love gives life. It is not enough to say 'I love' – love must be your innermost feeling towards every soul

you encounter. You must know too that your brother
or sister is striving towards the light, even as you are.

*

A pupil of the Master learns to avoid all argument.
The one who follows the path does not enter into
conflict. The wise one on the path enters into the
God-consciousness which is all around him or her,
and sees God manifested in every living thing, in
every form of matter. The wise one sees God in
every religion, and truth in everything, knowing
that nothing can be without God. He or she sees
the manifestation of God *everywhere*, in every event:
sees that human self-will alone causes the individual to suffer. The wise one sees the manifestation of
God's love even through human suffering, and sees
the love of God bringing all human sufferers at last
into the kingdom of happiness and knowledge and
love and power.

*Some more words now on this so-called discipline, for how-
ever joyful White Eagle may regard the discipline of service in brotherhood to be, it is not always an easy concept.
For instance, our self-discipline involves stepping outside
a great deal of debate precisely because that could lock us
into the physical world, and it also involves remembering
the principles of the Brotherhood even when we ourselves
feel that we have not been honoured, whether this is true
or not. Our ideals of oneness have to be greater than our*

need to defend position: while brotherhood will contain instruction in how grievances should be dealt with, harmony remains the primary aim of every brother. And sometimes that requires a considerable amount of work. Above all, we should remember that we are needed by spirit, needed as the gentle hearts through whom the light is brought to earth. The work of the Brotherhood is first and foremost to help humanity to evolve spiritually. The work of the Brotherhood is to increase the power of the heavenly light and to bring it even closer, but it is necessary to have channels right in a physical body and on earth. God needs this, the angels need humanity to become conscious of this life, this light of the Son of God. This is the only salvation for every human being.

If you are working earnestly and sincerely for the brotherhood of all, you must get above the material thoughts and clamour of the opinions of men and women. This is why, in the brotherhood, we have learnt that earthly people must endeavour to be non-political. Maybe you will not approve of our words. Nevertheless, the supreme thought in a brother or sister's mind is to unite in spirit, in the Christ Spirit, to serve God and humanity. When you are in the midst of the turmoil of the lower mental plane you are cut off from that supreme intelligence, that divine love. But brotherhood does depend on unity: as soon as you are out of unity with your brethren, too, you put yourself, for the moment, outside the chain of brotherhood. The white magic loses its power to operate if there is a weak link in the chain.

When there is discord in a group, or in a lodge, the masters withdraw. You will see in the world that many groups start with good hearts and good intentions, but they lose contact with that magical power. When there is dissension or lack of love, the magic goes and the love and the power of the masters goes too. In your brotherhood, always work for harmony. Know also that if you follow the true light, which is love, nothing can go wrong. Everything fits into place like the pieces of a jigsaw puzzle. You do the right thing. You obey the Law. God will do the rest. Remember, a sense of humour will save many a little difficulty. Be amused! You will see the twinkling eye of the Master, and if you see White Eagle with clear vision you will see that we often have a twinkle in our eye.

The final passage in this chapter is a reminder that though brotherhood has much to do with service, it also has to do with growth. In the meditation that follows, the instructions 'Feed my sheep' are effectively the final words of Jesus while on earth, from the end of St John's Gospel.

For the present we advise you to cultivate love, not only for your fellows, but towards life and life's conditions. You do not see why you should love difficult and irksome conditions. But this is exactly your task. Bear no resentment of the conditions in which you find yourselves, beloved brethren. Nothing happens out of order or by chance, and the great Law brings those very conditions in your own life which you *need* for growth. As you till the soil and fertilize the earth with natural manure, and tenderly plant your favourite flowers, so are you, a human soul, planted in the same tender loving way. When you realize this you will no longer resent the conditions in which you find yourself. However difficult, you will say, 'I thank Thee, O God; here may I grow to full stature, to finest beauty'. The wise man or woman will never question 'Why', but will know that the Father in heaven is perfect in His wisdom.

Become, so far as you can, the ideal which you must have of your master, and you will recognize him or her on the outer planes when you meet the one you seek. It is possible that you will meet your master in your sleep state, on the astral plane; you may recognize him or her when you know your own guide. It is likely that your own guide is one with your master. Do not get confused, but remember that though all masters are one, yet all are separate, like drops in the ocean. Do not seek a separate master – the Master is one; it is a plane of conscious life.

You may meet your master when you least expect him or her to be with you, but everything depends upon your ability to recognize that being. Did not one of your great American philosophers say, 'It takes a God to see a God'?

Look for love – godliness, and a great human heart; one who understands, one who can be happy and radiant and joyous, one who can still play with the children, and rejoice; one who has a keen sense of humour, and a twinkle in the eye, one who is full of life and joy and happiness! Yes, a great human heart and spirit ... in such a one you may find the master.

Peace be with you, and the joy of life be yours!

The Presence of the Star: a Meditation

There is a figure in the heart of this Lodge, so bright that the features are indistinguishable, but the form is there, though the features cannot be seen, in the centre of a blazing golden light. There is compassion and love pouring from this figure which can be sensed, and the figure takes the form of a triangle....

Now it takes the form of a six-pointed Star ... blazing, blazing, blazing, dispersing the darkness, gradually bringing law and order out of chaos. And the words, so clearly, so musically ring out.... '*Feed my sheep ... feed my sheep*!'

CHAPTER 7

Initiation into Service

One of the things the Brotherhood on earth seeks to do is to take the good thoughts of all human beings and concentrate them where they are needed. The amount of light generated by good thought is a quantity, a mass of goodwill that can be dissipated or enhanced according to the work we do to bring it together. It is particularly true today that goodwill is a kind of network which knows no international boundaries.

The passage that follows, however, was given late in the Second World War at the time of the New Year and is deliberately offered in its original form so that it relates to actual conditions pertaining, as a way of indicating the great importance to Spirit of work with the light on earth. The second passage, after the asterisk, was given at an even earlier time of great conflict and disorder among nations.

WE CALL YOU to fresh service. We call you to see that you put forth your very finest efforts on the plane of thought, on the plane of spirit. There is at the present time an accumulation of nebulous prayer and good intentions. It is the work of the Brotherhood to will the Will of God, and to direct the prayers of the mass of humanity into definite channels for the reconstruction of the life of humankind. In this you know that you will have the help of the angelic beings. It is their work and it is your work.

Your world today is in a state of chaos, and the chaos must be brought into order, into form. This is done through the will of those children of God, whether they be human or angelic, who have been taught to use thought power to mould the nebulous thought-substance of people on earth. The prayers and the good thoughts of the people will bring about victory over evil.

We remind you that the work done by this Brotherhood more than a year ago (indeed nearly two years ago) is today having its effect. Spiritual force takes a long time to manifest in these days, because the massed thought of ignorance holds back the manifestation of the light. Therefore you will see the grave importance of your service – now. See to it, my brethren, that henceforth your will is brought to bear upon this collective massed thought, and gather it, mentally, in a very definite manner and direct it into some channel which will serve human-kind. *Now*, each day (you may choose your time, but twelve noon is a very good time) we beg you, whatever you are doing, to call yourself to service, even in the midst of the world. Do it continually, all through the day, but do it particularly at twelve noon. If your thoughts are engaged on a mechanical task – well, it makes little difference, your mind can still direct the light.

Collect the good which other people are giving forth in their prayers, and direct it dynamically into the heart of humanity. Will, by the Will of God, that the leaders of the peoples shall be brought under the forceful influence of the Christ. If you will do that conscientiously and definitely, you will see miracles. The trouble has been in the past that you have all been half-hearted, fearful, anxious, depressed – but also we recognize that it is only through these mental and spiritual experiences of humanity that people learn their lessons.

So, my beloved ones, we greet you, on this New Year, with one word – *service*. Service of the spirit, service of the Great White Light.

*

Learn to survey your own life, as well as the life of the nations, with dispassion. You see a suffering humanity, yes – but you are looking at the picture too closely, instead of with a clear and true perspective. Great things are happening: a speeding up of individual, national and world evolution. You are being taught to look upon the changes in your world as resulting from the operation of law and perfect organization.

Simple and humble as little children! Commence on the inner planes, with the self within. Don't shout about peace, but *become* peace in your life. Cease to

143

fret over trifles. Know that those behind direct the course of your life, and the life of the world, with wisdom. Hold humanity always in the light. The efforts of those who understand the evolutionary laws of human life are called upon, are needed, to assist the building of the great white temple, the building of a great and free humanity.

Watch every step of your daily life. In brotherhood it is expected of you. Take no side in argument: do not say, 'This country is right, that one is wrong'. You have given up these things, these illusions. Take no side, press on with your work, being light, being love. The disciple must learn to work consciously with the powers of good, of God, for the advancement of the whole human family. Continual service to your brethren is the way.

What follows is a testimonial to the sheer power of what the Brotherhood seek to do. Reading or hearing the news often leaves us feeling powerless: this passage is the antidote, for it gives a whole new 'take' on the power of thought.

When White Eagle refers to a yogi he means not just a student of hatha *yoga, but a very special sort of being. For examples, see a work such as Paramahansa Yogananda's* AUTOBIOGRAPHY OF A YOGI. *The quotation about faith is from St Matthew, chapter 17.*

There are certain people who are known as yogis: we speak of the true and balanced and spiritually evolved yogi who is wise and beautiful; not all who follow the path of yoga are thus evolved. We mean those spiritually advanced men and women who have lived long on this earth, have seen the vision glorious and who have through repeated lives so trained themselves spiritually, mentally and physically that they have attained complete union with God, their Creator.

The yogi knows that the works of the white magic are produced by steadfast God thought. The yogi never wavers, never doubts, but holds the God thought so faithfully, so intensely, that he or she is expressing it in action and word. Do you remember the saying of Jesus, the greatest yogi in this present cycle, *If ye have faith as a grain of mustard seed, ye shall say unto this mountain, Remove hence to yonder place; and it shall remove*? But we have not faith – no, not even as much as a grain of mustard seed – that is the trouble.

The materialist denies the power of faith, and she says, 'No, impossible'. The materialist sweeps along his path of darkness and, like the Pied Piper of Hamelin, draws all the weak and faithless with him. And yet your doctors will tell you that experience shows thought to be a mighty power. It will change the bloodstream, cause fever and death, or heal the most fearful complaints. By thought the world was created, and everything on it was created through and by thought. Everything. People forget this, and conclude that things are made by hands, by machinery. They do not think deeply enough to find the true conclusion, that every material product is the result of thought.

We said at the outset that the positive God-thought of one individual had greater power than the negative thought of ten thousand people. You have it in your own power to test the truth of our words. By your thought you can affect your own body and your own conditions and circumstances, and remould your life. You can see the power of thought stamped on the face of every man and woman and child you encounter. You can read the habitual thought of the individual plainly impressed upon the countenance, the figure, the gait and gestures, the writing, the speech; what dwells inside a man or woman is expressed in every breath he or she breathes, in every word and act.

This is your world – but men and women do not realize this. We tell you that life after death is made up of your thoughts. The life beyond is the thought-state; it is on the planes of thought, and substantial they can be. Where you go to after death of the physical body is precisely decided by what you think. You will migrate to the state you have created by habitual thought, and through thought.

*

146

When the Wise Ones give us work to do, they do not always tell us how to do that work; they expect us simply to do it. Otherwise, dear ones, we should not learn. Work is given to you – then do your best, never turn away from the task which is given to you. Keep on and on and on. This is a test, my dear ones, through which we all have to pass; and when the task is most difficult, then it calls for all your endurance, for all your tenacity, to keep on keeping on. If a soul can pass that test of endurance, then it has learnt a great lesson, and may become conscious of unseen powers working for and with it in its task.

Do not run away from your difficulties. Stand firm and face them, otherwise they will crop up again and again. They will have to be met and overcome at some time. It is always wiser to face these difficulties; and material or spiritual, you will always find the cause *within yourself*. Be courageous, dear ones! Have courage to examine yourself honestly and truly, and you will find it a real help. This is a revelation which will come to you when you have the courage to admit and see weakness within.

Karma is the tool or chisel used for growth. Masons will understand perfectly what we mean. Karma is one of the tools which you, the divine man or woman, are using. Do not let your karma use you, but take your karma and allow it to perfect the rough ashlar of self. Your freewill is the God principle within, urging you upward. That which is called evil comes from the lower self, from the weakness of the flesh, and the shadows which your own weakness draws around you.

White Eagle has spoken a very great number of times about the one he calls Divine Mother, and there are several such passages above (see p. 52). The mother principle begins within the Trinity, but it is best to see Divine Mother as a being presiding over the creation and nourishment of form. In St John's Gospel (chapter 19), there is a moving moment when Jesus, from the cross, calls upon his disciple John to be as the son of Mary, his own mother; and upon his mother Mary to be as mother to John. There is a most beautiful symbolism behind this, which White Eagle explains in context in the book THE LIVING WORD OF ST JOHN *(see p.23). For the moment, let us see it as depicting how through the power of the Christ a human can be raised up, and stand as one fully expressing divine power.*

Here, White Eagle shows that Divine Mother also enables our work, because she raises us and enables us to develop higher consciousness.

The work you are doing in this brotherhood is so closely allied to the work of the Divine Mother. In her story is the mystery which lies unsolved by the human mind, the mystery of the nature of Jesus Christ. This mystery is to be solved by a deeper understanding of the Holy Mother. In the Roman

Catholic Church, worship of the Divine Mother is established, but this aspect of the deity has been lost in the Protestant presentation of the Christian teaching. In the future you will find greater and greater emphasis laid upon the spirit of motherhood. As we say, it contains a deep mystic truth and truth can only be unfolded a very little at a time. Some people long to know everything. The mind is avid for knowledge. It has to learn that it cannot learn through the brain, but only through life and through love; for love and life are the two magical powers which unlock the mysteries of the heavens and the earth.

When you are projecting the light to the women of the world, to the spirit of the motherhood of the race, do not think in terms only of the female organism; think of the spirit of the Divine Mother which manifests through all people, through men as well as women. It is that spirit of tender love and gentleness and humanity. This is of the Christ too and it is the saving power of humankind. Jesus was in fact a great illustration to the world of the feminine aspect of God. When you meditate upon the known personality of Jesus, you will recognize the gentle mother spirit manifesting through him. You will recognize the femininity.

We draw your special attention to this so that you will understand the importance of the motherhood of the race, because it is the Divine Mother who is becoming so powerful. It is this spirit of motherhood which is giving birth to the new age, and the work on the inner planes of all knowledgeable brothers is of great assistance to the invisible hosts who are working under the direction of the cosmic order.

You will see in the new age evidence of the traits of the gentle mother, the growing sensitivity to the traits of the soul, for the woman represents the soul of things. You will see the growth of soul power. It is now coming slowly before your notice, but in this new age not only will the mental body be stimulated but also the soul power, and instead of having a few so-called mediums or psychics you will find that all people will have soul development, the quickening of the throat and the heart centre. All will accept what is now a mystery and what is ignorantly denied by the world. They will accept the truth of these invisible forces that are working through matter to raise it to a higher rate of vibration.

'Walk lightly on the earth' is one of the watchwords we hear quite frequently today. Here, White Eagle gives another reason for walking lightly — or, shall we say, simply. A phrase he once used was 'with simplicity, humility and high endeavour'.

In the second passage, he reminds us that our brotherhood role is karmic and derives from spirit.

150

Give all. This does not necessarily mean give all your money: but give, brethren, as you have received. Give all the love, all the light that you have within you. Give it all; broadcast it every moment of your life. In problems at home, problems with your family, problems with your brothers, the answer is to give and give and give that simple light, that pure light of the Sun of God which is in your heart. So simple, but so difficult! This is the meaning of all that happens in the material world, and every man, woman and child will have to learn this lesson before they have finished their journey. Every soul will have to learn it because that is why the soul is here on this earth planet. . . .

When you truly, truly come into the work of the brotherhood you are faced with a question – God or mammon? In the ancient mystery schools the candidates for the brotherhood were told that they would have to be prepared to give up the world if they wished to serve God and enter into the temple of the Great White Light. In this modern age, you have a more difficult task than the brethren who came before you, because you are faced every moment with the clamour of materialism and the development of your mind. This intellectual development (which is quite different from the development of the higher mind) and the problems of modern life cause you to be very puzzled as to what you are to do.

You are puzzled as to whether you should be practical and keep your feet on the ground and look after yourself and material things. We would like to explain to you that giving up the world to enter into the world of God does not necessarily mean giving up material possessions. It is your attitude towards them that matters. You have to understand that whatever difficulty arises, whatever problem is before you, you must first and foremost give all your trust and place all your faith in God's wisdom and love. That is all it means.

*

Every brother has his or her own particular work to do; you are all as one, and no one is higher or better than any other, but you will all have your own particular quality of consciousness; you all have your own particular human quality, mental quality, soul quality, and you will be used always for the work chosen for *you*.

This is a subtle point, but one we would like all brethren to understand, because we notice that many brothers and sisters want to do what they think is right. You all have your own idea as to what you want to do, and believe me you sometimes are wrong! Sometimes you are better qualified to do other work, take another position, and so the attitude of a good brother or sister must always be, '*Thy* will, O Master, *thy* will be done in me, and through me'.

152

You will not always like that will to be done in you! We have seen so many dear, dear brothers and sisters pushing their elbows out and kicking their toes and fidgetting because they were not doing what they felt they ought to be doing, instead of waiting quietly, patiently, lovingly for their work to be given them. The Lord knows you, and the Lord knows the need for you in his particular part of the vineyard. Don't push your elbows out, don't get agitated because you want to do work which is not allotted to you.

There is so much to learn about brotherhood even in very simple ways of everyday life. To walk the path of brotherhood is like walking on the edge of a razor, because truth appears to be a paradox. You are learning how to keep your balance on the path.

We say this, dear children, with all love. The power of the brotherhood, the power of the Star, is magical. The magic of the Star is love, and only when a brother or sister is full of love for God and humankind will the magic work. The magic is not self-will, it is love. You will be called, you will be chosen, and you can be quite sure that the work which is given to you to do is given by the council of the masters in the lodge above, not by earth people. Be ready to go forward and do your work, and be content to return to your seat when you have finished it. This is one of the most important lessons for a brother or sister to learn and it all adds up to one simple word: humility — the magic of humility.

Do your work with all your heart and all your mind and all your strength, but don't hanker after someone else's. The brotherhood is like a jigsaw puzzle and every brother and sister has their place and fits in perfectly to the picture.

The fearlessness of a brother or sister is what really allows that person to love. Here, the second passage takes that thought further, and speaks of the quality of stillness — along with another quality, easily forgotten.

We are aware of the troubles which exist in the world and of the fears which fill many minds at the present time. Fear is the worst enemy. Indeed, we say that fear is humanity's last as well as first enemy. The man or woman lives in a physical body from birth to the passing out of the body, and the pall of fear — fear of ill-health, fear of loneliness, fear of war, fear of catastrophe, fear of disease — is the very shadow, my beloved brethren, which prevents the flow of the physical forces.

You have been given a physical vehicle for certain work and life on the physical plane, and the soul can only get knowledge and wisdom from this human experience. You cannot learn in the same way on the astral plane or higher planes as you can learn in your physical vehicle. God has created this beautiful vehicle for you, and what has to be done in your life is done by the grace and love of God. God sustains the physical body to enable the soul to gain experience while in the physical body. There is no need for you to lack anything that you need on the physical plane.

Sickness and disease are results of the hold-up of the spiritual forces. Many of you are spending your time and love on those who are sick and weary. You are striving to help them, and God passes through your instrumentality the rays of healing. But there is something more that is required: the touch, the word, the power from the aura of your spirit to the spirit of the one you would help. You cannot always make that contact because the one before you is not willing or ready, so that all you can do is give according to your power and the knowledge that is within, and if it is not received the Christ force will go in a circle and go back to the sender. So all healing and all good thought and all the effort you make to heal the one before you, spiritually, materially, and physically, is never lost. The good which is in you and which you send forth is creative and eternal and it works in circles for good and blessing of those who send it forth.

Life, death, and then life again ... all go to form the pattern. Overcome the fear of transition from the world of matter to the freedom of pure spirit. You do not know what you miss when you look upon death with fear and sorrow. We say this to you, my brethren, to enable you to do more to help the bereaved, and to help those souls thrown suddenly out of mortal life. Because this is part, and a very important part, of your work in this Brotherhood.

In the final, very meditative, passage of this chapter White Eagle gives us a vision of the one thought of as the master of the brotherhood. It is important to remember that actual appearance is unimportant to any master; the visual clues are only present to stimulate archetypal memories in us, and in fact we may all conceive the visage of masters in our own separate ways. Nor, maybe, is the master tied to one gender — in the same way as White Eagle earlier commented on the feminine in Jesus. Note the difference between the loving master of the brotherhood here, and the exalted being of the separate meditation that follows.

Try to feel the actual presence of the master (for there is a particular master behind the work in this place). You may not know him. But we would present to you his picture.... Conceive then a form of perfect manhood, a face tender in compassion and love, golden in colouring; deep blue the eyes, and the aura a mixture of blue and violet and golden light. But the master can be very human, more human than any one of you, for he has trodden the path that you now tread, and the very stones that cut your feet have cut his also. Conceive him, then, not as some magnificent being, dwelling apart, but as one tender and true, feeling with you every hardship, every disappointment, knowing your weakness and glorying in your strength. Come into his aura, and learn to *love* … as he loves.…

And if he who is so beautiful, so great in spirit, can continue to pour his love upon you, in spite of all, is it very hard for you to give your little love to your brother and sister, and all living things? Strive to do this. But there is much to learn in the lesson of brotherhood: bear in mind, beloved brethren, that love divorced from wisdom is no longer love. The love–wisdom ray is indivisible. You must learn to distinguish between true, impartial and compassionate love, and emotionalism which will sweep you off your feet and destroy love. To love is to give the highest and truest within you to your brother or sister; to love is to give the light from your own soul, the white light of Christ. This is love.

Carry the picture of this master in your mind; those of you who serve in the work here are his pupils and his children.

The Christos: a Meditation

Forget your physical surroundings, as we take you in spirit to the cave of the Brotherhood in the world of spirit.... As you sit here, silently worshipping God, see the white-robed brethren seated in a circle. And into their midst there comes, slowly and gradually, an immense figure, a beautiful being with arms outstretched. The figure is so large that it touches with its head the top of the circle of light and with its feet it touches the lower part of the circle, and with the outstretched hands it touches each side of that circle. This scene, which is actually taking place, has a far deeper meaning than perhaps any of you know. That figure is the beloved Son of God. When brothers can put themselves *en rapport* with that figure of gentleness, love and power, they are filled with joy; and in whatever they have to do they feel the presence of that great mighty being, the Son.

You are part of that grand being. If you can realise that all work can be for the Master of Love, and send your thought to that great Being, you will absorb the confidence, the strength, the gentle power which will flow to you in the silence.

CHAPTER 8

Finding Strength from the Silence

The passages in this chapter can be read sequentially like the rest of the book, but they are particularly open to slow concentration and thus suitable for meditations, or for individual readings in groups.

The first might be entitled 'To be as the Master': this is a prayer that we may be used in service. White Eagle makes an assumption of human goodwill — every being, in its own way, longs to be part of the whole by serving it.

EVER IS WISDOM simple, and comes to humanity through the centre of every individual being, which is the heart. The nearest approach to the heart of wisdom for you is through the Grand Master of the World, whose light was manifested and still manifests through Jesus. Other torches have been lit to guide humanity in its search, but great light can be kindled in your heart through your observation and absorption of the Christ love.

It is not enough to say, 'Master, Master!' Rather you must be as the Master; for you cannot divorce action from the knowledge which has become yours. When you pray to be used in service, are you willing that this should be according to the Master's direction, according to his will, and not your own? You desire to work for peace, but how useless it is to strive for peace in the world if there is raging tumult inside your breast! Quench the fires of passion and desire, and peace will radiate from you and, as a flame, light other torches on the path.

Do you desire to know your master? Your master will first speak within your own breast. Until you can hear his or her voice clearly, you will not meet your master in outward form; but once the voice makes itself heard in the temple within, you will surely meet your master in the world without, and in physical form.

How can you best help humanity towards the universal brotherhood of the Great White Light? By seeking wisdom, prompted by the love in your heart; by learning to withhold criticism, condemnation; by seeing only the God struggling for manifestation in humankind.

You are needed. Of yourself you are nothing, but do not close the door through which the Great White Light can shine upon your suffering brethren. Be on the alert to obey the voice; hold fast to courage and a deep faith that the light can never be extinguished. All else may fail on this earth plane, but the light – Christ the Sun – will endure. For even as it was in the beginning, it is now: so shall it ever be, world without end.

*

It is good to bare the heart to the God within. We must seek sincerity. In other words, we must be true to our inmost self; we must analyze our motives, searching for any sign of selfish desire. This is the first step on the path to knowledge of the secrets of life....

Be at peace, beloved; work within the silence in your daily lives, contributing to the universal life, the love and the wisdom, which shall be revealed to you as you commune with God on the mountaintop. The pure in heart shall see God. Purity and simplicity are the keynote of true brotherhood. No one is great, only God is great; we are God's children, and so partake of that greatness, only within God's power, will and love. Only when the light of God shines from the altar of our innermost being can we truly participate in the purity and simplicity, and yet greatness, of God our Father and Mother.

The previous chapter closed with a sense of our ideal. In the present one we shall unfold a sense of how it is the silence, above all, that is our tool in going into the presence and finding truth.

What does a Master offer but love and openhearted truth? And how do we best witness such an example, other than in the silence? A later passage offers statements that may be used, in most cases, as affirmations; we would note that they often might be used as little meditations, too. In this passage, something seems to be coming through from an even higher source. Note particularly another passage here about the great Mother, and how the warmth of our care for humanity places us as the mother herself towards them.

No attempt through verbal definitions and explanations can truly reveal the secrets of the universe. You cannot understand by words, but only through soul experience: and soul experience is available for every human being in every walk of life. It all depends upon how you commune with the spirit, how you act towards your brethren, how you discipline the unruly lower self, how you live, and how you seek to attune yourself to the pure Christ Spirit. In other words, how faithfully you endeavour to bring the spiritual principles through into everyday life, their first foundation being love: real, kind, true love, and tenderness and understanding.

We know that your ideal of your Master is that of a man (or woman, it may be) who is all love, all kindness, all light, but who also possesses great strength, who is unshaken by the storms of life, like a lighthouse built upon a rock, upon which the wild seas of humanity beat. Unmoved, the lighthouse continues to send forth rays of light across the dark and stormy seas. The soul that has attained mastership will never fail to give forth magical white light into the world.

So when you hear talk about secret societies and hear of people rushing to join so that they will learn something others do not know, remember what we tell you – that the true secrets are universal. They can be shouted from the mountaintops. There is no need to enter any secret society to learn them. When your soul has evolved sufficiently, all secrets will be communicated, not necessarily by word of mouth, but in your heart, and by the ways of the Master, by the ways of God.

Sit in the silence and you will hear secrets whispered to you. Go out on the sunlit downs* with the sea rolling upon the shore beneath the cliffs, and listen with your heart. You will hear secrets whispered to you. Go into your brotherhood to give true service to humankind, to commune with your comrades in spirit, and you will hear secrets communicated to you, secrets of which it is quite impossible to speak but which come to you in your heart.

You will know how things happen, why things happen and how evolution is proceeding. And you will know where the key to the gate of heaven is to be found.... You will know how to insert that key and unlock the gates. You will understand the meaning of every ceremony and every symbol that you encounter in the temple of the holy rites. You will become acquainted with, indeed you will be the companion

---

*The downs of Southern England, systems of undulating chalk hills, touch the coast at various points, resulting in high white cliffs.

of, the angelic brotherhood who are ready to lift the veil and show you the very deepest secrets of nature and of creation, and of the life-forces in the earth, in the rocks, in the water, in the fire, in the air. All this you will know and you will understand the inner sacred meaning of the consecration of love, and you will experience the consummation of real love. You will follow the one path, my brethren, of real living, of the real expression of all the gifts which God has implanted in your body and mind and soul.

Strive to be real ... to be real, to be human and to be divine, and you will become aware, fully aware, of the vast temples of ageless time.

*

My brethren, we can give you no truer teaching than this. Intellectual gymnastics may be pleasant and you may enjoy them much as you enjoy physical exercise. But remember, you do not find God along that path in the way that you can find Him—Her through love, by feeling your heart expand to the extent of the earth itself and even beyond – so that you enfold all the suffering and sorrowful into your heart as does the great Mother, the Mother God. Think of the yearning of some mother-heart for her children! Then, instead, think of all the children of God – all men and women everywhere ... and then you – *you are* the Great Mother.

My beloved, think often of God; meditate upon

God many times a day like this, no matter what you are doing, when it is possible to open the heart and send forth this love without criticism to all humanity. This is the path which if persisted in will bring to us divine illumination, divine consciousness, divine vision, universal knowledge.

What did Christ say?

'*I AM the Way, the Truth and the Life!*'

'*I AM … I AM God within the heart;*

'*I AM God, the universal life.*

'*I AM everywhere;*

'*I AM in all things;*

'*I AM the Father and the Mother;*

'*I AM the Son.*

'*I AM the God, the life …*

'*I AM the way, the truth and the life …*

'*I AM the light and the joy and the happiness of life.*

'*I AM the peace;*

'*I AM the tranquillity;*

'*I AM the storm;*

'*I AM the stillness …*

'*I AM THAT I AM.*

'*I AM the beginning and the end …*

'*As it was in the Beginning; is now; and ever shall be, world without end.*

'*This I come to teach. I manifest through men and women according to their desire to love Me. No man or woman shall find Me except through the love and through the Son. I AM manifesting through all World Teachers, through all the saints of all time. I AM the one life, the only true light which lighteth the way for humankind on its journey to God.*

'*I AM....*'

So, my brethren, withdraw your minds from the outer world and enter into the ashram. Within you will hear the Master's voice. The sages have shut themselves away from all clamour, ambition and claims of the material world; they enter into the silence and find ... God. In the western world it is harder, but the end is glorious, and therefore we teach you to turn away from the market place and seek the ashram, the place of stillness, of all power. This is the way, the true way.

White Eagle goes back to the theme of simplicity, with which he began this chapter. On the occasion the next talk was given, and on many others in the London White Eagle Lodge, the sound of a bird — probably a blackbird — was heard singing outside the window above. The talk was given in the Second World War and many more intrusive noises must have distracted his listeners during those years — explosions, sirens and anti-aircraft fire. These things White Eagle never once mentions. Yet the little blackbird held his attention on many occasions — in its beauty, we think, he found it more real by far than the sounds of violence.

We do not like to interrupt the singing of our little

brother. His message is as clear to the pure heart as any human words can be. He is just rejoicing in his being; he does not reason or question – he just *is*. The trouble with human beings is that they are held in the meshes of material thought, which means physical bondage. Reason holds them prisoner. We say to each of you, use your reason – but beware of your reason, too, because it can hold you in bondage through many lives. Reason can bring self-destruction – and when we speak of self-destruction we mean spiritual death. Let reason be your sweet guide, but never your master.

Beloved brethren, humanity makes life so complex; it brings upon itself an avalanche of confusion, pain and suffering; it is driven by desire and by intellect, both of them enslaving you – and yet the way to freedom is so simple. The way is so simple that most people escape it, pass it by. It looks insignificant, and when people have it pointed out to them – their master within – they take no notice. They will not listen to the voice of their master: they only listen to the voice of self, and self expresses itself in many ugly ways: self-importance, self-love, wishing to shine before others. These things are of the lower self, but the God self, the inner light, does not wish to do these things. It is at peace, for it knows God is omniscient; it knows that there is only one path – such a simple path! It is a direct path to God. There is only one truth that humankind needs to grasp — one truth, and all things on earth and in heaven are then made plain.

The one truth is to know God, to be united with God. That is all.

*

Search for wisdom, true wisdom of the spirit, the wisdom which perceives the law of God working through life, which discriminates between the things which matter — the real things of life — and the unreal things which are transient, which are with us for a day and then pass into the unknown. Search for the wisdom that reveals the true life of God in bird and beast and flower and tree, in the stars and planets and in the great cosmic life; the wisdom that teaches the purpose behind every experience; the wisdom that teaches us to live that we may serve life and all creatures, and to leave this earth plane richer for our incarnation.

In the next passage, to the themes of silence and simplicity is added that of service. Although White Eagle here speaks of occasional failure, the context of his teaching is that failure does not really exist; all things are constructive in the teaching they offer us. By failure, he here means the things we judge ourselves for — and has said many times that it is just as important not to slay the inner being as to avoid slaying any other human.

Within the silence is the heart of truth; within the silence of the lodge, within the silence of your soul, the wisdom, the power and the love, the creative forces of life, gather upon the altar – the centre of the lodge, the heart.

Be still, and you will know no fear; be still and you will know the radiance of health in the soul. Be still and you will know the power that has created you.

May each recognize his or her potentialities for service. The ray upon which we work has taught us that the centre to be opened first is the heart, wherein dwells all love, all wisdom. All love ... all wisdom.... Let us first learn to still the turmoil and the storm that rages in the mind and the emotions, and then the Master, the Son of God, Christ the Lord, will rise within the lodge, and take command. We know that the one wish and aspiration of your hearts is to serve humanity. This you cannot fail to do if you send forth love. This does not mean where you choose only: every moment of life, *love*.

*

Do you not absorb understanding, and a quality of consciousness, from your contact with the silence? Have you sat in the silence, away on the hillside or in the meadow, and gazed before you into the ether, and seen (with what appears to be your physical but is actually your etheric eye) countless myriads of tiny flecks of light dazzling with vibration? Do you think that is an optical illusion caused by little flecks of dust in the sunlight?

You are wrong, if you have thought thus, for these little specks of light are the finer ether which is interpenetrating every form of life, without which you would not be in existence. It is the soul of the earth; it is the life-force, and it is this ether which the spirit people use to manifest to you. Without this finer ether we could not be speaking to you tonight, and it is through a method of controlling this ether and directing it upon a certain magnetic centre of the physical body, and permeating the etheric body of each man or woman, that we are able to speak to you from the spirit world.

Now realize that as you cultivate the awareness within your soul of the light of God, or the Christ spirit, so you must necessarily open the way for the greater inflow of spiritual knowledge into the centres of sensitivity in your body. It is perfectly scientific. And thus you become alive, a small radiant ball of light, a sun – in a minor degree, but a sun!

Silence is a sound in itself, but exists alongside sounds of great beauty. Harmony is not just the opposite of discord, it is perhaps the highest expression of creativity. The following passage, largely about <u>music</u>, is included here partly as a reminder that the concept of brotherhood owes a great deal to a teacher or master of antiquity – the great Pythagoras, *who is also said to have gathered round him one of the earliest recorded brotherhoods. Brotherhood, from a Pythagorean perspective, is a creation of harmony just like musical composition, with all souls blending in music.*

We find it difficult to talk about the beautiful truths of the higher worlds, since you can only understand the language of earth. We try to put into words something of the glory of the heaven worlds, but this is not possible. For this reason we desire your own soul to be attuned to the heavenly vibrations; you are helped in this by angels, and by your own teacher, and by the accumulative memory of the past stored within your soul.

The whole of the harmony of the soul must be quickened from the one central point in you and in us all; this central point is the spirit of God, the Triune Spirit of wisdom, love and power. This point must be touched if there is to be harmony in life, for this is the law of the universe and the individual. You will admit that life on earth is discordant; and after your soul has been attuned to the higher harmonies, when you return to the outer world you feel jangled, disappointed and upset by the crudities of life as lived by humankind in its present state of understanding. This very contrast between what you find in your group of service, or after meditation and communion, and the life of harsh ugliness, unkindness and unbrotherliness, indicates where the harmony of life originates, and where the true music of the universe is to be heard. It is within the soul, and the spirit is the musician, the performer, the conductor.

Music is mathematical. Music originates through mathematical calculation and conclusion; this is why the ancients had to train in astronomy (or astrology, as it was called), mathematics and music, because these three form the central trinity, or the basis of all the perfection of life. Without law and exactness, this world would be chaos. The Lord God, the Trinity of wisdom, love and power, which spoke the holy Word, calling order out of primordial chaos, was the creator of life on the planets and on the earth planet. Thus we might say that music is the creator of life.

It is a natural instinct for humans to seek the strains of music, however crude. When the soul grieves and when it is joyful, it finds expression in song; and from the beginning of time, through music, humanity has worshipped the Most High. All humanity, and the angel world too, forms part of the music of the spheres. The harmonies of life lie dormant within the human soul, and by its attunement to the divine harmonies, to the holy planets and the outer planes of the solar system, so the soul becomes a clear and true note in the universal harmony.

Each one of you has a note that predominates, according to the predominating planetary influence

172

in your soul. This means that in your aura you have a predominating colour too, for every note is expressed by a colour. Every planetary vibration is a colour. The combination of the seven notes of music, the seven colours of the spectrum, brings into being the one grand harmony, the one divine light, which is the light of Christ – love.

Love, then, contains all. Love contains wisdom and power. In the Trinity we seek the one predominating note: but if you know perfect love, you know wisdom; if you have wisdom and love, you are powerful and have poise. The three are inseparable – three in one, one in three is the divine fundamental note of music, of the harmony of life.

The ancients arrived at musical notes and relationships through mathematical calculations more profound than are understood by people of today. The calculation of the distance between the planets was one of their greatest studies and works. Absolute mathematical calculation of the heavens was the origin of music. You may go back into records long past, and find what is described today as crude music – weird sounds. You do not know how these sounds were arrived at by the ancients, nor what they may symbolize.

There is perhaps food for thought in what we have told you of the origin of music. When you listen to music, remember that the strains of harmony bring into play natural forces of the spirit which can be demonic or angelic. The demonic forms, although they appear to be destructive, have their part to play in the great scheme of evolution. Remember that God is omnipotent. The demons of life which cause disruption and inharmony and breaking down of creative force come to clear away the mistakes and apparent failures of men and women. Humans are as children, learning in a kindergarten. Coloured chalks and paper given to the children are often spoiled and useless. They are put into the waste paper basket. Then the demons throw the rubbish into the furnace but are only allowed to destroy that which humanity has made unworthily. Then angels again come and again bring the harmony of spirit into human life, and the worthwhile material is woven into a permanent structure or garment.

We have tried to convey in simple language an understanding of the process of creation and evolution, and the foundation of the harmonies of music in the soul worlds. Above all, you are a tuning fork. Strive to register a pure, clear tuning note. In daily life, be still and calm in your soul, so that you may vibrate in harmony with the music of the spheres. Thus you will be creating, and not destroying, the finer ethers in which you live – and live for others.

One of the great White Brotherhood, and a great musician, was the Master Pythagoras; to him the modern world of music owes much, for he taught his pupils about the soul harmonies, the heavenly planetary influences. He taught them wisdom and love.

We bless you all! We leave you in the deep peace of the eternal God.

Brotherhood can be seen in the work of a small group or in the ideal of the brotherhood of all humankind; but White Eagle reminds us that the whole of life — all space and all time — is one vast brotherhood because it is, in effect, the mind of God, the thought of God. As we discovered, early on in this book, White Eagle's view of human evolution is one that involves progression into consciousness of self, on into group consciousness and finally into divine consciousness. The role of brotherhood in training us for this now becomes apparent. Here White Eagle talks of our very life as being the greatest teacher we have.

It is a wonderful thing, life: it is wonderful to have been breathed forth from the heart of God; to be held in the thought of God, the mind of God. Yet everything and everyone in creation is held in the divine mind. Can you comprehend the extent, the grandeur, the power, the glory of that mind, which creates and holds the creative thought so that that thought becomes a living thing? No; it is beyond the finite mind's power to grasp. Some of you who are accustomed to meditation might have a fleeting conception of this profound truth.

The masters teach us that if we would tread the path of the mysteries, we must train ourselves to think accurately ... this is real, this light which is being generated by you, rising in you. See it in the form of a blazing Star. This is not imagination, but what you are creating by your aspiration, your will, by direction of your thoughts. What you have to realize in your meditation is that you are working with the *substance* of God, which is eternal.

When we are all attuned in heart and mind, the Star Circle, or the Christ Circle, is very close to the earth. Its work has been to break up the hard crust of materialism, and in this work you have participated in common with all humankind, for the sufferings of error on the earth have brought about disintegration and a breaking up of the hard crust of materialism which people had drawn around them. Now is the time of most vital need, for the balance has to be struck and maintained. For this purpose all truly initiated brethren are needed. Your work is not to accumulate facts and figures and theories, your work is to be up and doing and being and *living* the life of the true Star brother or sister. Such is one who has overcome the darkness in his or her own nature or who is making a valiant effort so to overcome. Great knowledge and power is as dust and ashes without the heart of gentleness and loving service one towards another.

*

This work continues through age after age, and the more advanced souls of the human race are the agents on earth for the Great White Brotherhood, through whom the elder brethren are able to work and to accomplish the plan of God for the building of what we may call the Great White Lodge. The Great White Lodge is rebuilt in every life cycle by the soul of humanity. Therefore the responsibility of those who are awakened and who know the way of life is indeed great; for upon them the masters depend.

Again we say, no man or woman can live in splendid isolation; all are linked in the grand chain; no soul can live unto itself, but when it persists in this selfishness, it diminishes in size and quality until there is nothing left, and the spirit, the divine spark, returns again to its creator. Therefore we see the inner meaning of the saving grace. We remember that Christ is in every soul, and works through the human soul to love and to serve all humankind. The impulse to love and serve, to be brotherly and give goodwill and kindness, is the saving grace of the innermost Christ. Through the human soul, Christ saves all.

For some, it is possible to work to serve the light in the comfort of a physical group and familiar surroundings, but others have to work on their own, seemingly. Of course no one ever works really on their own in brotherhood: but the

*individual path may involve developing the consciousness
to create a sanctuary at the etheric level, one which nonetheless begins to have the feeling of a 'home' or of a special
but very personal place. To develop this means that everyone
has, or even is, their own 'lodge'.*

Now we all, as a Brotherhood (speaking of the
Brotherhood in spirit), come to reassure you of the
reality of the Great White Light. It is within your
own heart, and as the flame rises within you so you
receive additional light and spiritual power from the
universal fountain. This light and power will never
cease as long as you open your consciousness and
let yourself slip into the ocean of universal love
and power. When you are weary, brethren, it will
help you if you will come in thought into your own
Brotherhood sanctuary, for we assure you that it is
never empty. It may be empty of human beings, but
it is never empty of spiritual beings, the four angels
around the altar, the assembly of White Brethren
who continue their service, whether you are there
or not. Come here in your astral body and you will
work with the angels and the White Brotherhood.

We pray for the time when you will all function
quite easily and naturally outside your physical body;
when it will be no effort for you to come here and
work. Cultivate the reality of this activity outside your
physical body. Train yourself to become accustomed
to such a thing. You will know it is true; you will be

alive with the spiritual power and the light. You will be as the initiate Moses when he became aware of the burning bush, the holy fire. This is the teaching which has come down the ages and every world teacher has endeavoured to give the truth of this fire.

Your Lodge in the heavens is a beautiful place, beauty you cannot conceive of in your earthly mind; it is a place of beautiful construction of light and colour. It is built in the form of a star and the arms of the star are composed of a spiritual substance more beautiful than alabaster, pulsating with light and colour; and in the heart of this temple the divine fire burns on the altar, which is a double cube raised upon seven steps, each step being related to the seven angels round the throne and the seven degrees of human unfoldment; to the seven windows of the soul, the seven rays of evolution and so on and so on. Do not conceive of the spiritual world as being cut and dried; it is fluid and all is continually unfolding light.

The panorama of the heavens is beyond your comprehension. We have told you before so that you may try to imagine it. Upon the altar there burns the divine fire which is representative of the light, and when the brethren are assembled in the lodge on that higher plane of existence, sometimes there comes the form of the One. We give It no name, but you know to whom we refer when we say the Perfect One, the Son, the King. And in that form you see absolute majesty and also humility and gentleness; and the power in that figure is the power of meekness and gentleness and love. This is our ideal, beloved brethren.

Finally, some deeper teaching on the silence. It is a touching memory to see the reference to 'Brother Faithful' as the author of a quoted prayer, in the final paragraph; for those who wonder who this individual might be, see the introduction. 'I and my Father are one' is from John 10:30.

In the process of cosmic evolution there is always a period of quiescence, or silence, a period when there is an inbreathing. You must all become well acquainted with such silence if you would know how to create — whether on the physical, the etheric, the astral, mental or spiritual planes of life. You must first enter the temple of silence. Moreover, you must be co-operative in silence. Never be exclusive. Remember, beloved, that no one of you can be exclusive; there must be co-operation and harmony on every plane of being, in every sphere of life. Therefore you must consciously train yourself to become a part, and yet the Whole. You must be the universal mind, and to attain to this consciousness, God has drawn for you a plan of life, a plan of the building which you are erecting.

We want you to become each day more aware of the presence of the unseen. We would emphasize the truth of the saying 'In spirit there is no separation', but first of all you must understand what you mean by this, what spirit is. Spirit is God-consciousness within you; and at the present time humanity is rapidly awakening to the awareness of the spirit within. Spirit is God; those who worship God must worship in spirit....

This means, beloved brethren, that within yourself is that wonderful love of God, and as you love in simplicity of heart, you are becoming conscious of the all-ness of spirit. As soon as ever you love, you are in touch with the Infinite. Because you are in touch with the Infinite, you are conscious of all love, and there is no separation. All power is yours, for you have become at one with God, the Father–Mother. And you can truly say, as did the Master of masters, *I and my Father are one.*

Do not regard the Master, the great hierarchies of angels, your departed friends, nor friends still incarnate, as distant from you. Do not look upon the masters as great beings far removed from you, great ones whom you are not able yet to contact – because by thinking thus you are erecting a barrier between yourselves and the masters. We would have you individually become conscious of the masters in your daily life.

Always, at any time, you can be in touch with the masters, and with God. And in the words of our dear Brother Faithful, we say: 'Thank God, our Father, for lightening our darkness', for in God we are in the light, in Him there is no sickness nor poverty nor death, all is eternal light!

A Meditation on the Many Forms of the Mother

Open your inner hearing to the grand orchestra of
heaven. Know that in the world of spirit is a sphere   *music*
of music – great companies of musicians clothed in
colours such as you know not on earth. Know that
they are with us now, that we stand in this sphere
of music. See the countless forms in multicoloured
garments. See the beauty all around us in the grand
temple of music – the glistening pillars of rainbow
light supporting the dome-shaped roof. And there
are gathered humans and angels, and those great beings who come from other planets in this solar system. Playing as children round the lake in the centre of this grand temple are countless nature spirits
– fairies, you may call them, in gossamer clothing!
– and even these little folk have their fairy instruments, and join in the grand orchestra of life.

Compare this reality with the discord of earth.
Why does earth's humanity fall so far short of realizing, in its own life on earth, this beauty of sight,
this harmony of sound, this glory of colour and life?
Because earth's humanity lacks the one grand truth,
that which is the cause of life as we have described it
to you in the heavens – it is love.

Carry with you this picture in life; may you be
all love and tenderness. Be merciful, for blessed are

183

the merciful; blessed are the peacemakers; blessed are they who are persecuted for righteousness' sake. Blessed are the pure and simple in heart. Therefore let us be kind to one another, always slow to anger.

CHAPTER 9

A Religion of Happiness

Much of this chapter will be about lessons that are learnt in conditions of joy, or in peace when it at last comes after a time of war. Today's large-scale problems, just as much as those of the past, require us to 'lift the veil of illusion' and see beauty behind conditions that seem incomprehensibly dreadful. Both the first two extracts date from a period early in White Eagle's ministry, when such issues were very strong. The phrase 'A Religion of Happiness' was the title of an early White Eagle book and is one White Eagle has used many times to describe the teaching he would offer us.

YOU FIND IT difficult in this modern age to appreciate the power of the spirit, the power of thought? But we say that the power of the thought of light, love and brotherhood will prove the saving of humanity. Clever brains will not save humanity, but are more likely to destroy it. Loving, faithful hearts will accomplish what clever brains cannot. Simplicity, true brotherhood: these are the forces which will yet redeem and save humanity and send it forth on the next higher spiral of human evolution. And whatever remains will be like a physical body that has died, a mortal coil that has been shuffled off.

Humanity will march forward. Send forth a ray of light and power until it reaches the darkest places on earth and into the spheres surrounding the earth. It will go forth, even as the Master himself, who still walks among his people, touching eyes sealed by blindness, making them see; touching hearts cold and chill like stone, and awakening them to life and beauty and love; touching misshapen bodies, causing them to be whole; touching angry hearts and causing them to turn to love; causing the nations to beat the swords and guns into ploughshares....

By this power alone will humanity go forward progressively, constructively, happily.

*

Do not imagine that suffering is the only way to attain to joy and freedom of the spirit. As we have already said, the path of suffering must be there for those who do not appreciate or respond to the love impulse in life. As soon as you can so make contact with the high and holy place within yourself that you can truly express love and beauty to your fellows, you leave behind your suffering, and enter upon joy and happiness. Through happiness you can learn.

Are you worthy to press forward on the path of happiness? You have the power to help your brother and sister to continue their ways in peace. May this be so. Peace comes when humanity knows how to use peace for the advancement of life, and not for selfish ends. Then peace abides. Ponder on that. Peace must not mean a period of ease and luxury. Peace must mean to each of you a time for progress. Bear that in mind also.

We cannot express in your earth language the glory of the heavens. You have no means of comprehending in words, even if we could find words to describe to you, the power and the glory of the heavenly hosts. You will only perceive that power when you can put into practice the power of the Star in your individual life. You cannot know these things by words or by pictures, but only through the emotion of love and brotherhood towards each other and all the world.

White Eagle has many times spoken of how closely joy and sorrow are related – opposite sides of the same coin, as it were. In clarifying this, the next passage may help. It was given in wartime, and is all the more remarkable for that in bringing a message of real and deep joy at such a time – but not, however, a joy that leaves responsibility behind. The quotation is from chapter 10 of St Matthew's Gospel.

Beloved brethren, there is so much sorrow and anxiety in the physical world at the moment that we would endeavour to speak to you this night upon joy, because there is so much to be joyful about, and you do not assist the human world by being drawn down into the vortex of depression and unkindness and selfishness and darkness.

There is a temptation to obey the stimulus of the lower self and the lower vibrations, but we would remind you of the great love of God; you have only to look into your own lives to recognize and see the wonderful love of God – to see how individually you have been preserved and guided and brought into the sunshine. You can look back over your present life and see many periods when so-called evil threatened you with sorrow and anxiety, but you can see that from that little shadow you have been led materially. You have not only been held and restored physically, but you have had implanted in your breast happiness and joy; you have been led into green pastures and beside the still waters of peace and contentment.

There is so much more joy in this life than there is sorrow. We want to remind you of this; were it not so, humanity would be completely depraved and would already be absorbed back again into the darkness. What is it that holds the balance so that human-kind is not completely destroyed, is not completely absorbed into negation, into darkness? It is the love of God, working behind the scenes of your mortal life, working through the angels, saints, prophets and seers of all time.

The Father in heaven knows your need … *even the very hairs of your head are all numbered*. There is more behind these words than the Christian has yet glimpsed. Jesus intended to convey to the Christian heart a message of peace … a message of strength. For when individuals become depressed and fearful, they become weak; there is no strength in them, no health there. We know that the trials of the phys-ical body can bring about depression and lowered vitality, but this lowered vitality and depression can be overcome by the spirit of joy from beyond, and by the light of the spirit, which must be *sought*. The windows of the soul must be flung wide, every day, to let in the sunlight of God's love. We know that sometimes the windows are barred and the latch is stiff and it is difficult to throw open the casement: but *it must be done*; the window must be flung wide so that the sunlight can pour into the soul.

You know how you feel on a sunny morning when the birds are singing and the soft winds are blowing through the trees and flowers? – you say 'Oh, it is good to be alive!' God's sunshine is bringing this in-spiration to you. But the spiritual sunshine is always there, no matter if the day is dark and misty – the sun is shining, though it may be obscured by mists.

This is why we wish to convey to you tonight this message of joy, not only joy and hope, but an *assurance* that God's love is omnipotent, omniscient, omnipresent, and it is only for the brother or sis-ter of our white lodge to receive it as a welcome and honoured guest, into your temple, your home (the physical body which is your home while you are on the physical plane). God visits you and does not come alone. God brings a great company of companions and brothers. Remember this, and be ever ready with your welcome to those honoured and faithful companions. In this way you are doing your work as a brother or sister.

God does not condemn His–Her children to death and disease. God intends these children to live happily, joyfully, like beautiful flowers, with their heads turned to the sun; and then, when the span of life is over, the spirit just withdraws from the physical vehicle and it is left to mingle with the dust of the earth – but the spirit is freed to continue to live a life of joy, perfect in God's kingdom. This is the life we would have you realize....

Before we leave you, we will give you a picture of a noble temple, built in circular form, with a rounded archway into the East. Look down this archway and see the form of Christ set there, within the arch of the temple.... Be aware of the grandeur and beauty of the building, a poem of architecture. Bathe in the fountain of light playing in the heart of this temple: every known colour is to be seen in the spray of light, and the spray of light looks like cleansing drops of the element water, which purifies, cleanses and heals the soul. Feel this spray from the fountain of life.

Let us now walk through the archway in the

west of this temple down into the gardens, walk on the green lawns, so green, so fresh, so soft ... see the masses of flowers grouped with perfect artistry on all sides of this garden....

We walk along the way and come to a flowing river. Oh, so clear that we can see the many brilliantly coloured stones in the bed of the river! Now, my brethren, let us recline upon the grassy bank at the side of the river and inhale the sweet perfume of the flowers, and hear the choir from the temple singing a *gloria*....

Now we rise, and we salute the Star! The symbol of our king, of Christ....

We come back to earth with renewed energy, refreshed, confident, singing in our hearts praise and thanksgiving for our creator, for this that we have seen is our true home and this home shall be established, through our own efforts, on the earth plane; and by our service to our humanity we shall lead many into this garden of refreshment and joy.

The next two passages might be found to contain further contradictions that are in reality not contradictions at all. The first speaks of earthly life and reminds us that there is an external perception we may hold, and yet the perception that comes in consciousness of brotherhood gives us a whole new level of awareness. The second passage is much more about the higher life, but how contact with the higher life can bring health to us all on earth. It applies to all workers for the light, however much it may seem to relate to White Eagle's own group of brethren.

In the first passage, the quotation is from Ecclesiastes 9:10.

If you would discover reality, look for it in life: in every form of life, and in human nature particularly; look for it in the counting-house and shop, in the bank, in places of amusement; in art galleries, in literature, in the human contact of wife, husband and child, and in family life. In every expression of humanity train yourself to look not at the surface, but at the sweetness and the beauty of the spirit that animates life.

We told you that you must all live in the present — *whatsoever thy hand findeth to do, do it with thy might.* If you enter a place where you are expected to enjoy yourself, enter into the spirit of enjoyment; give to your fellow men and women fellowship, and the joy of a spirit radiant with understanding and companionship and goodwill. Do not think it wrong to do this, that or the other. Never condemn: look, rather, at your fellow and say, 'He is good; I like him; she is honest, or she is kind'. Always seek for the truth, and in the one that you have hitherto considered unworthy or worthless, you will find God. Remember, the drunkard who crawls in the gutter may be greater in his or her love for God and humanity than the Pharisee in his robes before the high altar in the temple.

If you would seek God, look for God in the brother and sister by your side, no matter how crude they seem; and in the most crude God will be the most apparent if you, yourself, are quickened to the divine vibration. Did not the Master see in Mary Magdalene a woman who loved him? And yet the Pharisees would have cast her out, and would have wrapped their garments around them. Did he not see in the publican–sinner, too, the humility of God's own spirit?

Go forth into the world, my brethren, to cinemas, to places of entertainment, to office, workshop, school, factory, shop, and make up your mind to enjoy your contact with your fellow beings. Look in them for the beautiful, and behold! – you will find the Master by your side, speaking to you through the man or woman you had hitherto rejected.

Hold fast to spirit – and *be* love.

*

Be true. This is the essence of the spiritual life. You know that the note of the spirit is sounded on the higher planes of life, and the knocks which you receive in your everyday life are to test whether you can ring true. To ring true you must ring always to the note of God which is within you. You must respond to the tuning note of the universe. We want you to think carefully over this in all your dealings with your fellows. Ring true. It is not easy.

193

The passage that follows is from a Brotherhood meeting in the first White Eagle Lodge (Pembroke Hall, in Kensington, London) two years after it opened. On the Christmas tree there was an ornament in the form of a spider, and beneath it a large collection of toys given for children in need. It gives such a touching message about our human interconnectedness that it is irresistible to include it in this compilation. Although it offers a very local reference, the little scene and the image of the spider have a much wider implication.

It is followed by other rather lovely short extracts, in each of which White Eagle speaks quite intimately to his brethren as would any teacher to those with whom they co-operate on earth.

The gifts of the heart: do not deny your brother and sister the joy of knowing that you have given them a gift of love. You know as well as we can tell you that it is not the gift of the material world alone: it is the gift of the love from the heart which is important. How does anything in life matter more, if you can feel the throb and love of your brother's or your sister's heart as it mingles with your own?

And there on the tree is the spider, weaving its web. Yes, the web of life; all the little threads of life being woven into an exquisite pattern. All good — everything in life being used. Patiently the spider works; patiently must the souls of men and women work, using every fragment of material, every experience, to weave the whole, to build the whole in the heaven world.

We bless the tree; we bless the children who will receive the silver threads of light from this Brotherhood; we bless the givers and the gifts.

*

No one is ever permitted to see the extent of their spiritual efforts while on earth. They could not bear it. But when you are disentangled from all earth's toils, snares and delusions – then you will be permitted to see. Then you will be untouched by praise, untouched by blame, and you will be beyond all adulation. But the recompense, joy, reward, will be in your heart. This is your work today. God bless you in every effort you make, my brothers and sisters, my beloved ones, my family ... my children. God bless you and love you.

*

Do you understand, my dear children? Forgive old White Eagle calling you children, but you are to us our dear, dear family, and you have been our children in the long ago. You have grown up a little since then, but to old White Eagle you are still beloved children.

*

You are enfolded in the love of all the White Brethren: joyous, thankful and secure. All is well. There is nothing to fear. Take up your duties. Keep on quietly keeping on, day by day filled with joyous assurance, and walk life's pathway hand in hand and heart to heart with these radiant ones and with your brethren who work with you in their coats of flesh.

God will not leave you. Give your trust, that is all. The light within you, the inner voice, will tell you truly your duty; then do that duty. And look into the face of your Master without fear.

The love of the Brethren we give to you, voicing their wish.... *God bless*, God bless you.

Something about brotherhood reminds us of myths of old, maybe because other manifestations of earthly brotherhood date from more chivalrous times. The first extract below serves to remind us of the Arthurian quest for the grail, and the second takes us to the Cathar or Albigensian heretics of mediaeval times. In all three, there is the image of the cave.

And so my brethren ... there lies before you a quest. You must take the road alone, every one of you. No one can travel for you and hand you out the treasure. You must travel that road yourself. You must take the key from the inner recesses of your heart and unlock the door for yourself. But although you travel alone, you are not alone, for all the other knights are travelling too, in search of the same treasure; you can comfort yourselves with this thought, that all brethren travel the selfsame road, all meet the same obstacles, all go through the same fires in the end. So, though you travel alone, you are never alone, and in time you will enter through the golden gate, the Royal Arch, into the Kingdom of Heaven, as surely as the dawn follows the night.

May this be a message to you of hope and inspiration. As you move forward you are – consciously or unconsciously, as the case may be – drawing your other brethren with you. Do not take too much notice of flippant speech and words which pop out of the mouth and do not come from the heart, rather seek for the jewels which are given forth from the cave within, from the cave which holds the magic lamp, the cave full of rich jewels. Many foolish words fall from the lips of men and women; the brother does not hearken to these and the sister waits lovingly and patiently to hear the gems of the spirit which rise to the lips from the heart that is all love.

This power, this light, is the secret of all the ancient brotherhoods. It was the secret that gave martyrs the power, the confidence, the peace to face every ordeal, every torture. Remember what we have said to you about overcoming fear. This is part of the training of every brother and sister of the light. We draw your attention to the Albigenses, those humble and beautiful souls who went to their next life with smiling faces, without any fear of the torture and death which awaited them. They felt no pain because they had overcome fear. The physical body felt nothing because it was enfolded in the great light: the nervous system was completely under control. It is fear, fear, *fear* that causes pain, and this the martyrs of all time have demonstrated by their overcoming it.

With all love we hold you close in our heart. When you think of us, think of the temple in spirit, which is like a cave of light, and the Brothers of the Cross of Light encircled by Light with the Star shining from the centre gathered there; and you will feel their love and their power coming to you.

Be patient. All will work out. All *you* have to do is to tune in to the right centre and all your little problems, heartaches, disappointments will be put right in a far better way than you could imagine. Do not be disappointed, my children. All will come, in God's time.

Now goodnight, and God bless you all, my dears.

Some closing thoughts about perspective now. If only we could raise our angle of vision, so much that we do not understand, that depresses us, would be seen as no longer needing our concern. Our lives would be a meditation.
The time comes when we shall view the situation from the mountaintop. Now, many are in the valley – although some have commenced to climb. When we reach the summit, we behold the glory of the panorama which the divine wisdom has planned.

There are no loose ends, either in your own life or in the lives of any others. God's plan is exact, more perfect than any edifice ever built on earth.

We endeavour to pass through to your consciousness a greater awareness of the beauty of the spiritual spheres of life. This cannot be reflected in the mental body, but only in the higher vehicles, the true spiritual vehicle of soul consciousness.

Be still, and know God! If your soul can rest in stillness like a deep clear pool of water, it may reflect the picture of heaven, the picture of Christ, who dwells in heaven. Let us feel, let us know His joy. When you leave your physical vehicle, you pass onwards into the heights (or the profound depths) of bliss. You will need no language to express or to receive impressions from those whom you love; you will be wholly conscious of God's love, God's beauty, God's power and God's creation, and you will use your mind power to hold in place forms of indescribable beauty – a condition of creative life, a power which is being born within you while you are living on earth.

If you do not acquire it in daily life on earth, you cannot acquire it in heaven. It may sound as though we have given you a paradox. No one can become as a God who has not passed through the physical life, the human relationships.

So may peace dwell in your souls, and may your

souls acquire the stillness of a perfect lake. Nothing matters in life except this. You will have lost nothing, nor will any opportunity be neglected for you to make progress, and also you will give abundantly to the brothers and sisters by your side.

So may the peace dwell in your heart, and the light of heaven shine in you. We need you so much.

*

The blessing of the masters of light is now pouring upon you. If you are attuned to them, if you are attuned to the light, you have nothing to fear, nothing; but you must live in confidence, in faith, in hope, and you will be mounting the steps which lead you above the mists of earth into this eternal and glorious state of life, which we cannot over-describe to you in earth language. It is perfect, it is beautiful, it is all love, a state of supreme happiness and bliss. Even in the work which is given you to do, even when you are directed down to the earth again to help poor, struggling humanity, you are filled with the joy and the love of Christ, which is the supreme happiness of the human soul.

Remember that is how you proceed on your path. While you yourself are receiving the great blessing of this glorious life, you are passing it on and giving to your fellow beings something of the light and glory of God; you are giving healing to the mind and body of those who are your brethren.

In our final section White Eagle is perhaps showing us his own dwelling in the mountains where all is peace and all are in harmony.

Once again we come from the silent places to give you our message of brotherhood and goodwill, and to bring you inspiration and encouragement in this work of establishing, on the earth plane, centres of light and power, centres of the Star Brotherhood. The Star Brotherhood is destined to bring to humanity the great universal brotherhood, the religion of the new age. The Brotherhood of the Star is being instituted on the outer plane of life by the most ancient Brotherhood known on earth, as well as in the spirit world. If we watch our Star radiating its light, and drawing into its heart the infinite light of God, we shall see the Star as a living and yet ever-changing symbol; the Star being identical with the rose – the rose of love, which must be wisdom, for all love in its truest aspect is wisdom.

The work of this Brotherhood is in its infancy. There is a great field of service for you all, for the brotherhood must grow, and grow and grow. We want you to think about this, because we must move forward and spread the light of the spirit life all over the world. As humanity marches from the darkness of materiality, it will need the brotherhood to give it understanding of life's purpose and work.

Be at peace … be strong in your brotherhood.

Never doubt, never waver in your belief that all is moving forward towards peace and progress. Of those who have received much in this spiritual work, much is expected. So our duty is plain, is it not? Brethren of the Light.... Brethren of the Light....

*

These Star Brotherhoods which are bound to come into being across the world are the Brotherhoods also of the Rosy Cross, another name for the Brotherhood of Christ (Christ being representative of the God in human beings – the Father God manifesting through the perfect man–woman). The Brotherhoods of the Star, the Brotherhoods of the Rosy Cross, are the ancient brotherhoods who work to bring to humankind the simple knowledge of the Christ in the heart. The establishment of this truth in humanity will enable you to open your inner powers of clairvoyance and clairaudience, enabling you to touch worlds beyond the physical plane, and to be a vessel for the living Christ, a channel through which the cosmic rays of healing may flow.

We see good springing up on barren ground when we see societies, simple groups, simple bands of people working in humility and in sincerity to learn of truth and to radiate this truth into a materialistic life. Let us not say, my brethren, 'Lo! We have the only truth, and our brother or sister across the way has not the truth!' Let us prefer to remember that God dwells in the heart of every one; that every human being will open to God and receive truth according to his or her capacity, and the conditions in which he or she lives, and the plane upon which the one is qualified to work for the service of humankind. All people who are working to break through their darkness and deadness of materialism are doing their work.

But there are those who can go even a little beyond this, and can come into conscious contact with the spirit life, and hold communion with inner groups of adepts and Masters, and thus work with greater power among humanity. Then let us so work, and let us open wide the door to the spirit of love.

*

And now, dear ones, may we go forth into the world of the human, joyfully, radiantly happy. As we have received, let us give. Happiness: happiness ... and joy! Be not cast down. Life is radiant, and all that is discordant will be overcome. Time bears you all onward, forward, upward, to the life made perfect, and glorified by your Father–Mother in heaven.

A Prayer of Thankfulness

We raise our hearts in thankfulness to God, being duly conscious of our blessings.

We thank God for the blessings of the angelic ones; for the sweet and beautiful communion of spirit. We thank God for the revelation we are daily receiving of divine beauty in life; in the love of friends, in our human companionships. We thank God for the fragrance and sweetness of the flowers, and for the service of the countless millions of nature spirits who carry the vital fluid to nurture the life of the plant.

We thank Him–Her for the law and order which prevail in heaven and in the creations of God on earth. We thank God for the service of our brother, our sister. And above all we bow in humble thankfulness for the gift of divine life and for the light revealed to us through the Son, who is Christ, whose divine essence is implanted in our hearts.

May we so think and act in life that we give love to our brother and our sister. Being ever mindful of the great calling which has come to us, we give love – our contribution to the great plan of evolution.

Index

205

THE WHITE EAGLE LODGE

The White Eagle Lodge is based on the profound yet gentle philosophy of White Eagle. Through his teaching we receive encouragement on a path of love, tolerance and service towards all life: a path which offers the development of inner peace and the awareness of our eternal, spiritual nature.

There are many groups throughout the world, and they can be found by contacting the main centres given below, which are centres for brotherhood work and offer services of healing, meditation, spiritual unfoldment and retreats.

White Eagle's teaching is offered in the printed and electronic books of the White Eagle Publishing Trust (www. whiteaglepublishing.org), alongside CDs and other publications.

Readers wishing to know more of the work of the White Eagle Lodge should contact us at **www.whiteagle.org** or at

**The White Eagle Lodge, New Lands,
Brewells Lane, Liss, Hampshire GU33 7HY.**
¶In the Americas, please write to
The Church of the White Eagle Lodge
P. O. Box 930, Montgomery, Texas 77356
(tel. 936-597 5757; www.whiteaglelodge.org;
in Canada, use www.whiteagle.ca)

¶In Australasia please write to
The White Eagle Lodge (Australasia)
P. O. Box 225, Maleny, Queensland 4552
(tel. 07-5494 4397; www.whiteeaglelodge.org.au).

¶By email, contact us at
enquiries@whiteagle.org (worldwide)
sjrc@whiteaglelodge.org (Americas)
enquiries@whiteeaglelodge.org.au (Australasia)